the library

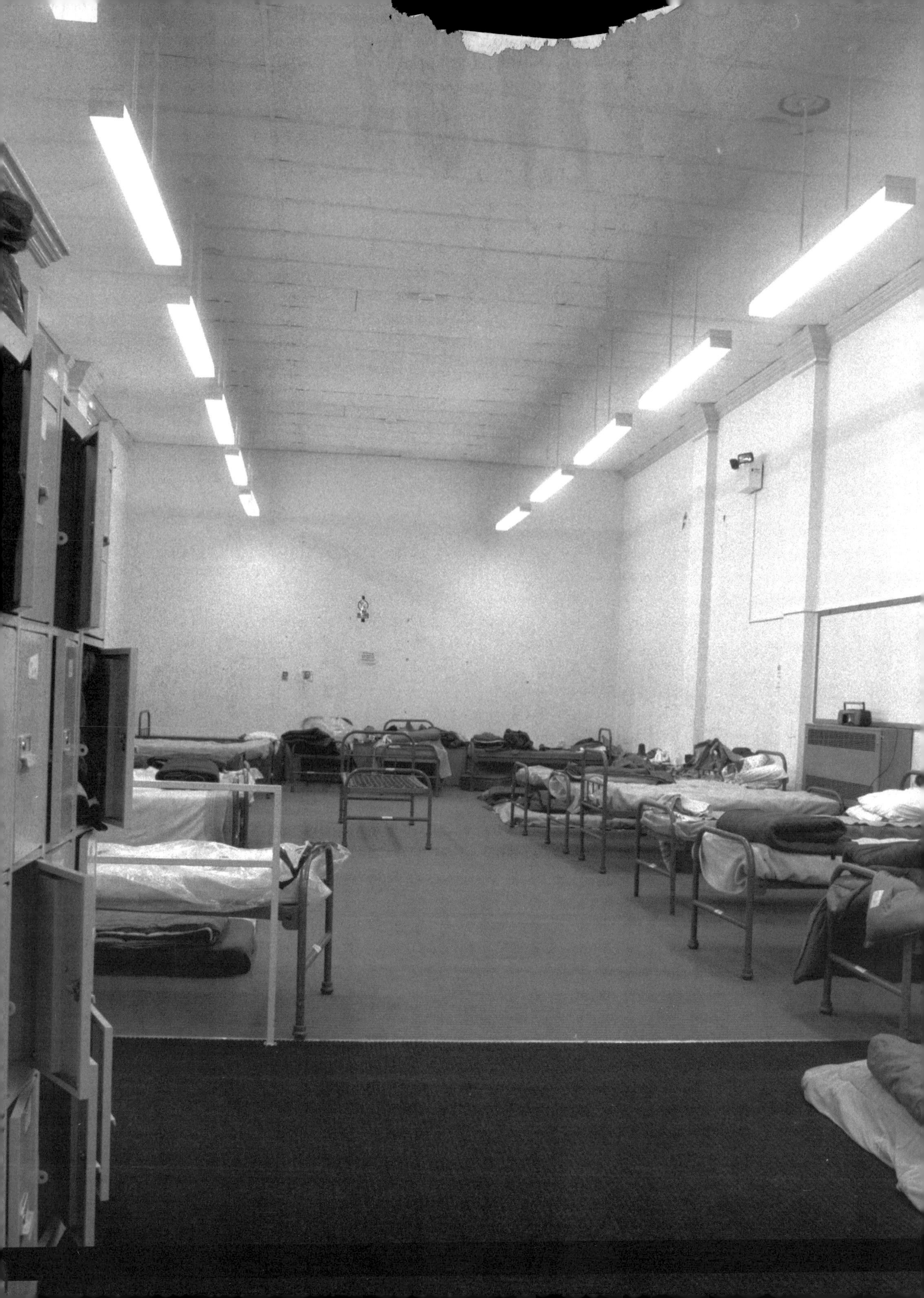

FIRE EXIT

Performance Research

A Journal of Performing Arts

Performance Research is an independent, peer reviewed journal published by Routledge for ARC, a division of the Centre for Performance Research Ltd, Cardiff, an educational charity limited by guarantee. Performance Research acknowledges support from The Arts Councils of England and Wales, De Montfort University and Dartington College of Arts.

Performance Research welcomes responses to the ideas and issues it raises and is keen to consider proposals for articles and submissions. Please address all correspondence to:

Clancy Pegg
Journal Administrator
Performance Research
Market Road
Canton
Cardiff CF5 1QE
Wales, UK

Tel. and Fax: +44 (0) 1 222 388848
Email: post@perfres.demon.co.uk

Performance Research is published three times a year by Routledge, 11 New Fetter Lane, London EC4P 4EE UK
A full listing of Routledge journals is available by accessing http://www.routledge.com/routledge.html

Enquiries concerning subscriptions should be addressed to the Subscriptions Department, North Way, Andover, Hants SP10 5BE, UK
Tel.: +44 (0) 1264 342755 Fax: +44 (0) 1264 343005
For sample copies contact the Subscriptions Department or email: sample.journals@routledge.com

ISSN 1352–8165

Annual subscription rates:

UK/EC:	Institution £80	Personal £29
US:	Institution $115	Personal $44
Rest of World:	Institution £84	Personal £31

Members of the Centre for Performance Research (CPR) will receive Performance Research as part of their membership. For further information please contact:

Adam Hayward
Centre for Performance Research
8 Science Park, Aberystwyth
Ceredigion SY23 3AH

Tel.: + 44(0)1970 622133
Fax: + 44(0) 1970 622132
Email: cprwww@aber.ac.uk

Design: Secondary Modern
Typeset by Type Study, Scarborough, UK
Printed in the UK by Bell & Bain, Glasgow

FORTHCOMING ISSUES

Issues 3(1) and 3(2) of Performance Research will be entitled *On America* and *On Praxis* and will appear in the Spring and Summer of 1998.

On America will respond to the powerful presence in contemporary culture of aesthetic forms and political strategies derived from North America. Counterpointing *Letters from Europe*, the issue will address the use and abuse of images of and from North America, the deconstruction in performance theory and practice of North American art, film and performance, and the presentation of America as genre and fiction. With contributions from theatre-makers, artists, theorists and critics outside North America, as well as those working on the cultural and aesthetic fringes within the Americas, the issue will debate the influence of North American cultural products and practices, providing a forum for debate over cultural hegemony and displacement, identity and aesthetic practice.

On Praxis. How does place affect performance praxis? How are geographical, cultural and artistic identities created and sustained with/in different places? How have colonial pasts, and the ways they mark and are mapped in the present, affected the performances produced there - not only in thematic ways, but in the making processes themselves? In Australia, for example, performance owes much to the colonial past and present: to a psychology of edges, of enforced comings and goings; of 'empty spaces' at the heart (out-back), sites for projected imaginaries and dis/appearances; and to a history of repression and genocide. How are such aspects expressed in performance practices?

ESSAY COMPETITION

In order to encourage new writing and new writers Performance Research is establishing an annual writing prize competition. The winning essay will be published annually in the Spring issue of the journal. The competition is open to anyone who has not published previously in a peer reviewed journal and is aimed at emerging writers, artists and graduates. Submissions can be made in the writer's preferred language.

Full details of the competition can be obtained from Clancy Pegg, Administrator, Performance Research, Market Road, Cardiff, CF5 1QE, UK. The closing date for the 1998 competition will be 1 September 1998.

The essay need not be linked to the journal's specific theme but should address contemporary practices or contemporary investigations of performance practice and its history. The essays will be judged by a select committee drawn from the journal's Editorial and International Advisory Boards.

SUBMISSIONS

Performance Research is a peer reviewed arts journal published three times a year which addresses contemporary performance research and practice internationally. It aims to promote a cross-disciplinary exchange of ideas; making connections between theatre, dance, music, time-based and live art. The editors are interested in receiving submissions and proposals from artists, independent writers, critics and academics working in these fields and in other disciplines. We encourage proposals using visual, graphic and photographic forms, including photo essays, original artwork for the page and mixed media submissions as well as substantial articles and reviews. There is no payment for articles except in the case of commissions for which funding may be sought. It is the responsibility of authors to seek permissions for all visual material.

Proposals may be submitted on one sheet of A4 containing an abstract, proposed word count and description. Unsolicited articles may be submitted for consideration by email, on disk or double spaced in hard copy. Detailed guidelines for preparing text will be sent either on request or on acceptance for publication. Proposals are considered at least nine months before publication.
Proposals and articles, including book reviews, should be sent to:

Clancy Pegg, Administrator, Performance Research, Market Road, Cardiff, CF5 1QE, UK.
Email: post@perfres.demon.co.uk

Volume 2 No. 3. Autumn 1997

On Refuge

Editorial

PLAYING HOST

What follows is a list of associations, readings and ideas generated from contributions to *On Refuge:*

home, haven, harbour, port, shelter, homelessness, destitution, sense of self, identity, language, culture, ethnicity, body, text, family, community, time, temporality, temporary dwelling, hut, box, repository, relic, offertory, convent, church, monastery, dispersal, history, tradition, faith, group, tribe, suburb, migration, migrant, journey, stranger, friend, pedestrian, walker, way marker, position, spot, reckoning, stigma, compass, chart, map, wandering, road, immigrant, transit camp, dormitory, van, alien(ation), the walk, the pilgrimage, where one is, sharing a presence with others, lived experience, 'the actual world in which we live' (Krzysztof Wodiczko), close of day, prayer, ritual, love, soul, cocoon, breast, the body as a house, source of solace, retreat, Kabinett, safe, property, boot, 'geopathology' (Una Chaudhuri), I, self, exile, 'you must leave the modest refuge provided by subjectivity' (Edward Said), emigre, traveller, nomad, gypsy, no hiding place, nation, land, ethnic group, country, town, city, neighbourhood, locus, locale, patch, manor, haunt, hotel, home: 'shelter and prison, security and entrapment' (Una Chaudhuri), sanctuary, asylum, shelter, stronghold, 'refugees are people in need of such a place' (Andrew Quick), the legal process, station, cell, castle, fort, place of resistance, pagus: enclosed field, page, pagan, territory, terrain, in the wild, domestic/contested space, a roof over my head, location, hut, hospice, hospital, a room of one's own, a place to stay, lodge, dwelling, nest, house (public/private), local, cottage, garden, paradise, Eden, heaven, corner, ward, hostel, bed, place, site, sacred site, Persephone, underworld, hell, haunt, hunt, move on, hounded, dogged, Diana, snicket, gulley, sneck, alley, close, seam, margin, strand, tunnel, protest site, utopia, different areas, hole in the wall, in camera, library, index, archive, geniza, file, dossier, codex, stage, screen, scene, space (theatre/cyber), site, ground, specific geography, diaspora, fugitive, untouchable, refugee, outcast, refuse, flight, time-frame, dream, work, dark wood, forest, cave, womb, carapace, shell, dystopia, desert, wasteland, boundlessness, emptiness, boundary, net, political/geographical refuge, taking refuge in the voices of others, 'a wish for safety in an unsafe world, a certainty for those who may be exiles in the country of their birth' (bell hooks), conditions for survival, story, narrative (one's own), book, text, word, script, closure, silence.

The idea for an issue on refuge emerged from conversations between the editors and contributors to the conference on tourism at the Centre for Performance Research in Aberystwyth in September 1996, in particular with Rustom Bharucha and Norman Frisch. We'd like to thank them for originating a concept which has generated such rich and provocative material. We'd also like to thank the many other people who have contributed and shaped this issue, some of whom, but not all, are included here.

Ric Allsopp
Claire MacDonald
Cambridge, 30 September 1997

Open Transmission

Krzysztof Wodiczko

An edited transcript of a talk given at the Institute of Contemporary Arts, London as part of the series 'Spaced Out 3' – Smart Practices in a Complex World (March, 1997). Born in Warsaw, Krzysztof Wodiczko lives in New York City and is head of the Interrogative Design Group at the Massachusetts Institute of Technology (MIT). An innate interdisciplinarity underlines his work, which originates from a training in industrial design. His overriding concern is the relationship to art, design, technology, ethics and psychology. His works *Poliscar*, the various *Projections,* the *Homeless Vehicle* and *Alien Staff* underscore the notion of art as a renewed form of communication with an emphasis on ideas about exclusion and strangeness in public space. The communication instrument of the *Alien Staff* and the discourse between objects and users is a compelling subject Krzysztof Wodiczko has been focusing on in recent years.

The city operates as a monumental stage and a script in the theatre of our way of life, perpetuating our preconceived and outdated notions of identity and community, preserving the way we relate to each other, the way we perceive others and ourselves. An intense presence of historic monuments, advertising, communication media and urban events merges with our own daily personal performance into one uniform aesthetic practice dangerously securing the continuity of 'our' culture. Media art, performance art, performative design: they must interfere with this everyday aesthetics if they wish to contribute ethically to a democratic process. They must interrupt the continuity of existing social relations and perceptions well entrenched in the theatre of the city. Such arts, using the words of Simon Critchley in 'Ethics of deconstruction', should 'interrupt the *polis* in the name of what it excludes and marginalises'. To preserve democracy one must challenge it; one must challenge its symmetry with an asymmetry of ethical responsibility.

• ***Alien Staff*** **in use, June 1992. Barcelona, Spain. Photo: Galerie Lelong, New York**

The issue of sharing a permanent presence with other people has already been raised here. Permanent presence, or the presence of the other, suggests establishing some kind of communication with another party in order to cross barriers, walls, distances; or breaking down the alienation or estrangement between two different groups. Yet there has not been much said about the actual world in which we live. It would be a great delusion to assume everyone is in an equal position to share, to open up towards the other, to communicate his or her own presence and existence, to learn from somebody else's experience and to accept

Performance Research 2(3), pp.1-8 © Routledge 1997

the presence of the other. This is definitely not the case today, in an era which has been called by the United Nations the 'migration era' – an era of international xenophobia or a fear of the other. This is also an era of uneven social relations affected by uneven urban development; an era of urban struggles, of survival through resistance as in the situation of the homeless or of street children born into poverty, hopelessness, violence; or of people who live with HIV infection, and many other marginalized and alienated individual beings, groups and populations. These people are definitely not in a position to share or even make their experience publicly known.

If we are talking about technology, then we must also think about communications technology. What is the position of communications technologies in the troubled communications breakdown that we are experiencing today? If we are so divided, then what is the meaning of an interactive situation between me and somebody else in order to work together, communicate or share things? If new forms of alienation are emerging today, forms that are yet to be discovered and studied, that's where I see the relation between ethics and aesthetics and technology. The more clearly I see it the more dissatisfied I am with my own work, which definitely still needs to absorb a lot of issues. I realize how behind I am in terms of the technological options we have, and the great possibilities that are there. When I speak with my colleagues in the Media Lab at MIT, I realize how late I came into the field of technology. There is already a new generation of people (especially undergraduate students) who are much better equipped at programming than are graduates or researchers. There is an incredible gap between those opportunities and the new responsibilities that they bring. It is in this situation that I am trying to present my work, which will perhaps inspire younger people to push it much further. I am trying to catch up with them; and they are hopefully trying to catch up with me in this area of art, of technological ethics, an ethics of cyborgs, an ethics of interactive environments and so on.

This photograph was taken by a photographer trying to grasp exactly the problems that are at the centre of my work as a designer – which is how to confront the communication gap, and the absence of or the need for something in between; for example, between the couple on the righthand side and the person on the lefthand side.

• *Encounters with Immigrants*, 1992–1993. Photo: Galerie Lelong, New York

Our strangeness is a strangely familiar secret, an uncanny condition which, when kept in the ideological cave of our subjectivity, can explode against the presence of the actual stranger. For those in transit, the state of being a stranger accumulates as an experience with no form, language, expression, or rights to be communicated. It thus becomes a dangerous psychic symptom as Julia Kristeva has called the condition of the migrant. Between the speechless pain and despair of the actual stranger, and the repressed fear of one's own strangeness (see in the couple on the right), lies the real frontier to be challenged.Can art operate as a revelatory, expressive and interrogative passage to such a frontier? Can it be an inspiration of, a provocation to and an opening act for a new form of communication, a new form for a non-xenophobic community? Can it provide an iconic object, a symbolic environment, an interface, with which to create or design such a reconstructive psychocultural project? Well, it is clear that the person on the left is not equipped to deal with this framing, colonizing, intimidating gaze. Nor is he in any position even to accept his own experience of crossing, trespassing and all the process of ethical and political survival, of living through it all and opening it up to find the form and the language, and to present it, expose it, announce it to this couple on the right, who obviously are not open to hear it.

So some equipment, some 'thing' in between him and himself is needed, first as a kind of psychological object, a new form of what D. W. Winnicot might call a 'transitional object' – an object that will allow him to play and achieve a distance, perhaps even an ironic distance, from the painful and impossible experience, in order to stand behind or next to his own experience and somehow open it to the couple. The couple need the object as well. For they cannot confront the presence of a stranger any more than they can confront their own strangeness, which is well repressed and hidden in their unconscious. They would prefer to expel the stranger, rather than accept him and thereby recognize their own strangeness. If, however, there was some kind of strange object between this person and them, they would focus on the strangeness of the object first, somehow putting aside for a moment the presence of a stranger. Perhaps in this intermediate moment, through this intermediate object, they might more easily come to terms with some kind of story or story-telling, some kind of performative experience, some kind of artifice, something artificial enough for them to accept the reality in a step-by-step way. I think that's what Freud and Kristeva meant when they were hoping for an artifice to help people come to terms with 'uncanny' strangeness. Of course they would want to establish a playful distance from their own fears through an artefact. That object does not yet exist; or rather, I have not yet managed to construct one successfully. I only attempted to do so and this is an experiment which probably will last quite a long time.

Such an experiment is a risk worth taking. The city is worth nothing if it is not open to strangers or the estranged. Technology or design is worth nothing if it cannot create such an opening. Each time the experience of a stranger is understood and heard, each time such acts occur, the city wakes up and comes back to life. It brings back hope for all of us if the city is a place of hope for the stranger. To heal one estranged speechless soul in the city is to heal the entire city. My role is to contribute to a therapy for the city and for its speechless actors. The instruments that I design are an attempt to do this. My interests in psychology and technology merge as they do at MIT; but somehow social ethics is not yet a powerful component in this merger. At MIT my role is to bring this component as a part of my art and my design.

My first experiment was a very simple attempt to reactualize so-called 'primitive' technology. A walking stick, the ancient technology of the transient, the messenger, a migrant or a prophet – a staff with specially designed code of interchangeable carvings – could become a symbolic inscription for migratory experience. For example, being deported (expelled from a new country) three times would be articulated through three forms attached to the staff; or if someone spent one year in transitional camps, or someone worked illegally for a year or two, those things could be carved or sculpted on the staff. Of course that idea needed to be abandoned very quickly since all of the Departments of Immigration – which are *de facto* Departments of Anti-Immigration – would have learned very quickly about this 'secret' code, and no immigrant would risk using such a walking stick openly.

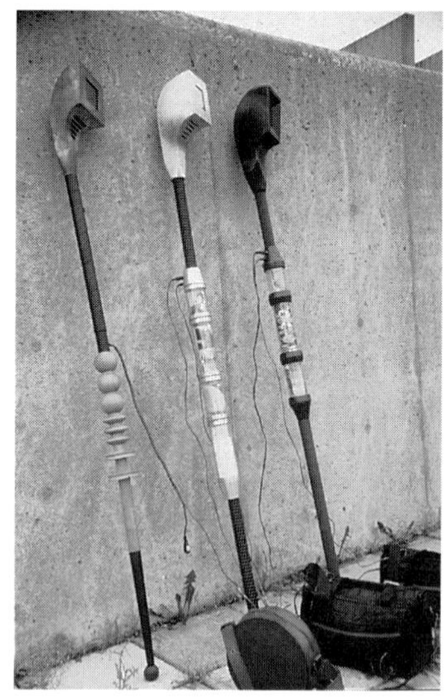

• *Alien Staff*, early models, 1993. Photo: Galerie Lelong, New York

At the top of this walking stick, called the Alien Staff, there was a video monitor and a loudspeaker which would represent the speaking face and the voice of the stranger. Using this walking speech-act instrument, a stranger, a story-teller, would feel he or she was perceived as a respectful and articulate actor in today's urban landscape. In this way the stranger could be reinforced by his or her 'porte-parole', as a companion, a confidant. There would now be two of them: the stranger as a character and as an actor. The prerecorded and well-edited speech – the story-telling – could be broadcast with the disturbing, comically disturbing presence and speech of the actual person who recorded it. The relation between the stranger, his or her media image and anybody on the street – the interlocutors – would possibly create a complicated discourse in which the stranger could disagree with what was prerecorded, because every time the story-teller speaks, the story would be different. The interlocutor could then ask questions related to the lower part of the *Alien Staff* – the history of displacement inscribed there – and the third person would come and start responding to the discourse with larger questions, questioning the questions, questioning the discourse and speaking on behalf of 'we' rather than only 'me' and the 'other'. This would create a political, critical and ethical field where both the interlocutor and the stranger, by referring to what was prerecorded and what was broadcast, could actually take up an external and critical position to it.

• *Alien Staff*, early models, 1993. Photo: Galerie Lelong, New York

At the next stage of the experiment, I realized that I needed to replace the carvings of the lower part of the *Alien Staff* with interchangeable transparent containers: containers for sacred relics, important documents, objects of historical value for the stranger. The stranger is treated and at best tolerated as someone who does not have a

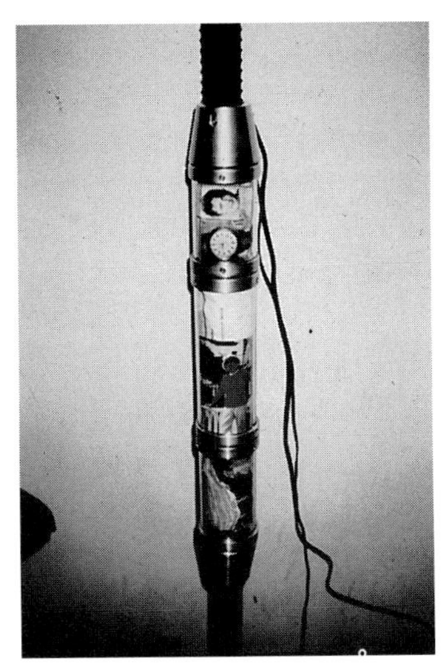

• *Alien Staff*, 1993. A reliquary section. Photo: Galerie Lelong, New York

history and must use story-telling, magic, song and other forms of performance and entertainment to insert his or her own history into the official culture; to propose himself or herself as a history. The issue is, what kind of history? The history of the time before crossing the border, or the history of the time after crossing the border – and I am emphasizing the history *after* one has crossed the border – that is, the history of the entire population, society or nation. This history is a performative kind of story that will eventually be distorted and absorbed by the grand national mythology and the city's monumental narrative, only to be challenged again later by another stranger.

The recollection of past experience infused in the present, in part creates a completely new history of the present, a critical history of the present. If I go through all the miseries of the past five or ten years, I must reuse them to imagine that this is going to continue; that the future is going to perpetuate that misery for myself and for my children. Therefore I – an immigrant and a stranger – am announcing what is wrong today. My utopia is based on a refusal to accept the place in which I am – a new concept of 'no place' – utopia. Utopia – that is a place that is unacceptable; and the hope that is born from this unacceptable experience is extrapolated into the future as another side of this utopia – so that the future will not repeat the injustices and catastrophes of the present and of the past. This concept of recollection, of remembrance, of critical reactualization and critical history is located somewhere in between Friedrich Nietzsche and Walter Benjamin. According to Stephan Moses, Benjamin suggested that the process of progress should be replaced by the process of remembrance and recollection. His utopia was functioning as the hope lived by the mode of the present, rather than as a projection of an ultimate social solution. I understand all immigrants as prophets, as prophetic peoples who through their disturbing performance and recollection of their present experience are each day announcing a better world for all of us. 'The Messiah interrupts history', says Benjamin.

• *Alien Staff*, 1993. Immigrant relics. Photo: Galerie Lelong, New York

These are the relics of a Polish exile living in Brooklyn who went through hell working day and night without documents and as a slave, as a domestic labourer, for a woman, the oppressor. The exile had no choice, terrorized to the point where she entertained the idea of committing suicide, or giving up the job and going back to Poland, all of which were equally impossible solutions for her. She survived this but she kept it to herself or to be precise, to her unconscious. She never really spoke about all of this with anybody. When I suggested this instrument to her she rejected the possibility of 'using it' on the spot. Mentally she needed 'to destroy' this instrument – the *Alien Staff* – in order later to accept it step by step and perhaps in the end even to become addicted to it. At first it was a perplexed reaction on her part. She rejected this project and at the same time she was allured by the possibility of exposing the history of her experience to a world ignorant of it. She also felt a need to share this with somebody, as well as with herself and even with her own consciousness. The process of video recording – of recalling details, trying to find documents and other relics, editing the story, translating very often from one language to another, speaking in two languages to the video camera – finally began. The same stories are different when spoken in different languages and on different days. To put it together, to concretize it in some synthetic way, is also to release the incredible load of speechless pain and responsibility for carrying all of this inside as a secret, as a uselessly hidden testimony to truth. Once the story is next to her, her strangeness is estranged from her in a healthy way; she sees and hears it now at a distance. She can know now that her anger and alienation are contained there (the psychological container is important here) and now she can be open. She can be very polite, she can negotiate between herself, her prerecorded double, the other person and the third person. She can also reserve her right to disagree with her double – her *Alien Staff* – at any time. As one rabbinical scholar said: 'The one who believes the story is a fool but the one who denies the story is a wicked non-believer.'

It is a myth that immigrants can understand each other. In fact there is a world of disagreement and antagonism between them – as much as there is a world of disagreement and antagonism inside of each immigrant. The boundaries and de-militarized zones inside the mind of the migrant are in the process of shifting; they are unstable, so in a way the possibility of internal conflict is as close as the possibility of external conflict among the different ethnic groups, and of course between each of them as individuals and the rest of society as well. This is why I am thinking that the *Alien Staff* can be expanded and absorb more contemporary technology, allowing strangers – their 'operators' – to communicate with each other electronically when they 'broadcast' and speak. At the same time they could provide a communication service as social aid for the larger immigrant population and everybody else, assuming that, for example, some of the operators, immigrants, would become agents, angels (*'l'ange' ou 'l'agent'*) or messengers who could then visit or explore different areas of the city where immigrants live. Such 'angels' would not only open up their own experience using the *Alien Staff* but also establish a trust – play and trust are interconnected according to Winnicot – to such a point that they could then transmit back and forth questions and advice; the questions would usually be legal ones, but could also be ethical ones to the communication base (the xenological base run by xenologists – immigrant experts on displacement), existential philosophers and legal advisers. Such an *Alien Staff* as a network is probably a very important option since many of the immigrants are not in any psychological, economic and social position to seek help or advice on their own and take advantage of their rights, if they still have any.

Alien Staffs were used in Barcelona, Warsaw, Helsinki, Rotterdam, Houston, Brooklyn, Marseilles, Paris – used by many people in many places even though there are only six of them. They can be shared and their containers and video-tapes are interchangeable. Confidence is a very important result of many of the conflicts, once one is prepared to open up all of this within the situation of the studio. A video camera is very patient. But then to accept this is another story. Once all of this is accepted it opens a new possibility: of thinking about one's own identity and participating in an experience and a life that are much richer, much more complex, than is the case for those who never cross the borders. Then the confidence and respect become a motivation for an action, or a speech-act, which is much more critical and demanding or provocative. It might perhaps reach the point (as in this case) where the person is invited to a TV station and appears on the national news. On occasions (and it has already happened twice), immigrants appeared on the official TV screen armed with their personal televisions, with both virtual and actual well-prepared statements, stories and visions.

• *Alien Staff* in use. Jagoda Przybylak, New York. Photo: Galerie Lelong, New York

• *Mouthpiece* in use, 1995. Helsinki, Finland. Photo: Galerie Lelong, New York

So those are the three models historically lined up. The next generation of immigrant instruments, called *Mouthpiece* or *Le Porte Parole*, is not for everybody – but only for those who really want to use it. This is not an artifice positioned next to the stranger. This is a cultural prosthesis which can help the stranger him- or herself to become a powerful artifice, perhaps a cyborg. This equipment is to be used by those who are extremely angry and determined to speak. But also by people that feel more 'cyborgian' than others. A 'cyborg' is a cybernetic organism – a hybrid of machine and organism – a creature of social reality as well as a creature of fiction. Social reality is linked to social relations, our most important social construction, and to the world of change and technological development where, as Donna Harraway was saying, the 'distinction between science fiction and social reality is an optical illusion'. On this basis the immigrant is in fact partially artificial and partially natural. It is also possible to say that once one becomes or is forced to operate this way, then maybe, as she said, 'dehumanisation is so inevitable that we might as well learn to like it'. If we can.

Of course the emphasis here is a prosthetic device. A prosthetic device not only is like an additional part or a replacement for a lost body-part but also empowers or extends the ability of a human or an animal. In this sense the 'cyborg' analogy is very close to the experience of migrants, and, as Donna Harraway also suggested, to women and other groups that are marginalized, silenced and oppressed. There is no way back to the 'lost land' or 'paradise'. In the proposed *Mouthpiece*, the combination, at the same time, of the deprivation of rights – speech rights – and the reinforcement of speech ability is ironic enough to let us find some kind of analogy to Donna Harraway's concept of the cyborg, which she called an 'ironic metaphor'. This gag – this loud-speaker – like a cyborg, takes irony for granted.

These are my hopes and my ideas. My design and organizational projections have not begun to materialize yet, but more and more is possible. Right now at MIT we are experimenting with a version of the new *Alien Staff* that is further developing or creating possibilities for artistic virtuosity. Gesture is of course a very important part of what is happening around this 'sacred object' . Strangers assume 'baroque personalities' according to Kristeva: overemphasizing things, accentuating, full of gestures, in order to compensate for the lack of adequate communication, and also abilities. And 'locals' seem to be immobile, completely opposite, making no attempt even to exchange a gesture. As the stranger becomes a non-stranger, the non-stranger must become the stranger, and somewhere half-way a new communication, a new community, is possible.

Coming back to the new version of *Alien Staff*: the antenna here is probably not necessary but is an 'ambient' and important symbol of the possibility of a transmission between or among each of the instruments and the base. The larger form of the head of this instrument is something to do with the need to reinforce sound – the large speaker, which can actually be more effective in an urban environment. Also new containers are being tested, so one could show or conceal what is inside: there are two options. But most importantly there are electric sensors being used here. This means that hand gestures towards each container can speed up speech 'switching' on the particular story – related to particular personal relics. It can modulate in a variety of ways to make it more or less hysterical, comical or strange, depending on the virtuosity that it demands on the part of the stranger – performative virtuosity. Those metal components are actually functioning sensors – all of this technology was developed in the 1930s by the Russian inventor Theremin who invented an electronic musical instrument named after him and operated by gestures. The Media Lab at MIT has further developed this system using new mini-computers, programs and micro-chip technology in this and other new instruments to increase performative quality. Story-telling will become new art and new craft. It took many months for Joshua Smith of the Media and Physics Group at MIT to complete the program for this instrument. I realize only now how long it takes to work with this new technology and new research. Two years is a very short time when it comes to programming and experimenting with new interactive equipment. So I am behind my schedule! But the new instrument, the new *Alien Staff*, responds with its stories and their variations to many gestures already. The *Prophet's Prosthesis* is coming soon!

‘A Path Is Always Between Two Points’

Andrea Phillips

> When I was teaching at Cooper Union in the first year or two of the fifties, someone told me how I could get onto the unfinished New Jersey Turnpike. I took three students and drove from somewhere in the Meadows to New Brunswick. It was a dark night and there were no lights or shoulder markers, lines, railings, or anything at all except the dark pavement moving through the landscape of the flats, rimmed by hills in the distance, but punctuated by stacks, towers, fumes, and coloured lights. This drive was a revealing experience. The road and much of the landscape was artificial, and yet it couldn't be called a work of art. On the other hand, it did something for me that art had never done. At first I didn't know what it was, but its effect was to liberate me from many of the views I had had about art. It seemed that there had been a reality there that had not had any expression in art. The experience on the road was something mapped out but not socially recognised. I thought to myself, it ought to be clear that's the end of art. Most paintings look pretty pictorial after that. There's no way you can frame it, you just have to experience it.
>
> (Tony Smith in interview with Samuel Wagstaff Jr, quoted in Fried 1967)

Recent dialogues on nomadism, diaspora, journeying, flight, mapping, space and ‘non-space’, site and ‘non-site’ have by-passed the pedestrian precision of the traveller. This particularity of ‘placing’, reconfigured by more generalized theories of ‘passage’, condemns geographical and historical specificity in favour of transitory, fluctuating, psychic experience. Such systematizations of ‘route’ constitute a convenient postmodernism, seeds of which can be traced in Tony Smith's evocative statement made over forty years ago. And whilst the ensuing ‘deterrestrialized map’ has been beneficial in its support of an ambiguously authored and ‘hypertranslatable’ imaginary, its trope of ‘charting’ (or indexing) has become uncoupled from the difficult directionality of real-time navigation.

What could be seen as a new type of sublime – the sublime of unrepresentability, of the constant in-between – is a refuge from the real that few artists seem to inhabit with the ease of their philosophical translators. In particular, artists who utilize performance present us with the ambivalence of physical reality alongside such constructions of ‘around the real’. Here, I will attempt to unpick some of the assumptions made in this ahistorical non-space by looking at the practice of four artists whose work throws specific light onto the political diffidence encoded within such a system. Two of these artists – Francis Alÿs and Gordana Stanisic – use walking in their works, whilst two – Danielle Vallet Kleiner and Penny Yassour – attend to the process of travelling and the physical contradictions of cartography.

Walking is a practice that literally grounds the map. Over the last few decades artists have used the activity of walking to remind their audience of the difficulty of retaining a practice that is located both historically and geographically within the social and engaged with debates concerning performance and ‘objecthood’ within the museum or theatre. Walking has many physical and emotional references: to ‘escape’, to enforced and poverty-stricken migration, to diasporic and coerced movement, to

Performance Research 2(3), pp.9-16

• *Istanbul–Helsinki (La Traversée du Vide)* (43'), Danielle Vallet Kleiner, Documenta X, Kassel, 1997. Videoprint: D. Vallet Kleiner

leisure, to health, to protest. These references have been taken up by artists in many different terms: Louis Aragon, Guillaume Apollinaire and André Breton all used the metaphor of walking the street-markets of Paris to emphasize the dreamlike quality of surrealism; Guy Debord wandered through the same city in order to highlight its spectacular nature; Vito Acconci attempted to 'get down to the street' to escape the gallery; Marina Abramovic and Ulay walked the Great Wall of China in a social act of healing; Merce Cunningham, Yvonne Rainer and Ann Halprin trained their dancers to walk rather than pirouette; Krzysztof Wodiczko used the image of a walking stick to highlight the displacement of migrancy in the USA (see his article in this issue). Following the lead taken by Michel de Certeau in his analysis of spatial strategies (de Certeau 1984) and picking up on some of the terms used by James Clifford in his recent writing on fieldwork (Clifford 1997), I hope to indicate how such a pedestrian practice might intervene physically in the problematically constructed but highly seductive 'in-between space' of recent theory.

Danielle Vallet Kleiner's video installation *Istanbul-Helsinki (La Traversée du Vide)* comprises a long, intricately constructed documentary of the artists' journey across mainland Europe. The film consists of a mixture of monochrome images of ships and coastlines with highly colourized road shots (the camera hanging amateurishly out of the side of a truck or a car, catching images that range from Soviet-inspired statuary and monolithic civic buildings to schoolchildren in playgrounds, seeking shade from the sun, and bustling ports). Many shots are subtly digitized – the colour contrast of sun and shade exaggerated, the pixilization of seascape made painterly – in order to confuse temporal representations. Sitting watching the work for half an hour, it becomes impossible to locate the imagery historically: pre- or post-communist; warship or battered tourist transport? The soundtrack, which ranges from Massive Attack to Mozart, is historically just as ambivalent. Occasionally, the camera focuses on a fragile silver disc pasted on to a wall – the side of a church, a school, a cinema, a railroad. At the 1997 Documenta in Kassel, Vallet Kleiner's installation was placed in a small mission room on the city's main railway station and accompanied by more fleeting, high-speed images interspersed with the news and advertising on two large overhead TV screens on the main concourse of the station.

Since 1987 Vallet Kleiner has been placing and then leaving silver leaf images across Europe; these images are filmed or photographed and left behind on contested sites as testaments to access, authorship and ownership. Not in themselves indicative of the violence of their surroundings, they become highly charged because of (or in spite of) their positionality. It's impossible for the viewer to know whether or not she actually made the trip; whether the footage is taken from home movies 'before the wars' or whether the buildings, ports and statues

• *Istanbul-Helsinki (La Traversée du Vide)*, Vallet Kleiner, 1997. Videoprint: D. Vallet Kleiner

that we see are those left standing. The pedestrian aesthetic that she employs points the viewer to the installation's outside: that of the station building, the 'mission' in which the video is watched. But what time is being looked at? What place is being looked at? How is the viewer to judge the specific but possibly fictionalized passage from Helsinki to Istanbul of the film's title in relation to the station: a place constituted by the business of starting and ending journeys?

In 1977 Rosalind Krauss highlighted the increasing concern amongst artists for the work of modern art to inhabit both space and time. In the influential publication *Passages in Modern Sculpture* Krauss analysed the shift of sculptural concerns as one that was both ideological (moving away from monolithic representation) and couched in a growing recognition of formal and intellectual interdisciplinarity (Krauss 1977). Whilst in 'Art and objecthood' Michael Fried used Tony Smith's experience on the New Jersey Turnpike to question the experiential, temporal theatricalization of minimalist sculpture ('There's no way you can frame it, you just have to experience it': an antithetical statement in Fried's world-view), Krauss chose the term 'passage' to signal a critique of Fried's essay. A passage, with its multiple connotation of architectural construct, use-value and physical activity, signalled the opened-up, fluctuating, performative space of sculpture for the author, who cited the work of artists engaged with the expansion of the 'field' of sculpture and its relation to dance, pedestrian activity, 'real time' and the environment outside the gallery as passages of possibility; possibility also dependent upon the uncommodifiable, 'unframeable' nature of the work.

Walter Benjamin, an increasingly influential figure in Krauss's later writing, used the terminologies of passage in a very different way. Whilst no less metaphorical, Benjamin's 'passages' were physically and politically literalized in the pedestrian arcades of *fin-de-siècle* northern Europe. Benjamin encountered them on foot: these glass and ironwork constructions linking buildings of the city together suited his project of revealing the ideological basis of history through the close examination of everyday life and its objects – objects found on a walk through an urban arcade. So for Benjamin the passage was both a contemporary problematization of the 'smooth' run of history and an archeological site: a dialectical space of frozen dreams, faded legacies of aspiration and bargain commodifications.

Between Benjamin's idea of the passage – a place for looking, thinking, gathering evidence, stopping, starting, discussing – and the postmodern in-between passage, there are several contradictions. Benjamin's passages contain the evasive but incomplete critical histories of the future. The postmodern passage becomes an all-encompassing spatial and temporal zone of possibility. Passage as a convenient metaphor for an uncomplicated mixture of *topos* and *telos*. But rather than the literal floating signifier of rootlessness often quoted as one marker of postmodern *flâneurism*, Benjamin's passer-by walks though the guarded space of the arcade, from shop-front to shop-front, 'theatre' to 'theatre', scene to scene, amassing a critical relationship to his or her spatial and temporal inhabitance.

The differences between these positions have implications for someone using the terms of nomadic, diasporic travel. James Clifford points out that the *flâneur* is constituted racially and in terms of gender by the ease with which he moves through urban space and takes up this nebulous public positionality. Analysing the positions of two figures in relation to the *flâneur* – the anthropological fieldworker and the transgressive informant within the 'field' – Clifford presents another complexity to Benjamin's 'botanising the asphalt' (Benjamin 1979). Like de Certeau, he sees the 'field' as a set of 'discursive practices' that are at once constituted by their directionality (where the fieldworker has come from, whether the field is actually constituted through migrancy). He replaces transglobal with *translocal,* emphasizing the difference between anthropological and travel encounters and, to a certain extent, begins to write through mobility towards the more resonant contemporary problems of diasporic coercion. Clifford's field is itself a place that is neutral and 'safe' only through historical and political creation.

Penny Yassour's installation at the Museum Friedericianum in Kassel as part of the 1997 Documenta included *Sealed Cape (Acephalus)* (1994), a 1938 German railway map, cast in thick silicon rubber and draped in a hump on the floor. The shape of the work bears a canny likeness to a famous photograph of Joseph Beuys, covered in a felt blanket, performing *Coyote, I Like America and America Likes Me* at the René Block Gallery in New York, 1974. The map is unreadable, inarticulate, impotent, reversing or reclaiming the routes that, at the particular historical juncture they were drawn, had an horrific usage. Through the work the artist recommends that we look carefully at the omnipotence of mapping; of the controlling aspect of hyperreal cartography.

As long as I'm walking I'm not choosing
As long as I'm walking I'm not smoking
As long as I'm walking I'm not losing
As long as I'm walking I'm not winning
As long as I'm walking I'm not making
As long as I'm walking I'm not knowing
As long as I'm walking I'm not falling
As long as I'm walking I'm not painting
As long as I'm walking I'm not hiding
As long as I'm walking I'm not counting
As long as I'm walking I'm not adding
As long as I'm walking I'm not crying
As long as I'm walking I'm not asking
As long as I'm walking I'm not believing
As long as I'm walking I'm not talking
As long as I'm walking I'm not drinking
As long as I'm walking I'm not closing
As long as I'm walking I'm not stealing
As long as I'm walking I'm not mocking
As long as I'm walking I'm not facing
As long as I'm walking I'm not crossing
As long as I'm walking I'm not changing
– I will not repeat
– I will not remember

(Alÿs 1997)

The pedestrian offers a dialectic of passage. At once travelling, the walker is also involved in a disjointed viewing, a partiality; a nomadism that is based on stopping, starting, constant decision-making. To walk is literally to re-place one's body in an actual sense and yet to be involved in an activity closely associated with magic, healing, penance, pilgrimage and transcendental flight. Opening up a space only to close it a moment later, walking at once offers a boundlessness and a boundary: the road is marked through praxis, in opposition to endless landscapes, by the precision of the feet.

Francis Alÿs, a Belgian-born artist living and working in Mexico since 1987, uses walking as a research activity, incorporating elements into gallery-based installations and performances. The text here is taken from one pasted on to a wall in the Whitechapel Gallery, London as part of the Antechamber exhibition (1997), in a work made specifically by Alÿs for that environment, forming a small detail in an installation of large sign-paintings, found objects, pencil and ink drawings.

Writing on Francis Alÿs, Cuauhtenoc Medina notes a reluctance to inhabit the in-between:

> Alÿs's position seems tailor-made to start that intellectual mechanism [of the postmodern as *melange*]: an ex-architect from Belgium, a migrant to Mexico, establishing contacts, mediating between shattered aesthetic poles, producer of dialogical experiences . . . all is there. But not as the performance of an iconographic fusion and an institutionalised *mestixaje*. His acts and objects would want to maintain themselves at a convenient distance from the formulation of an 'identity', in the more general sense of the term. . . . his work is organised around adventures of interrelation which imply obstacles: choosing between the closest distance between two points, the most intricate route.
>
> (Medina 1997: 54)

Alÿs also works in collaboration with a *taller* – or workshop – of sign-painters who reproduce his small, unfinished pictures and sketches on a larger, more 'efficient' scale. These works, in the hard professional airbrushed colours of enamel and gloss,

• *Multiple de três unidades*, 1994, Francis Alÿs and collaborators. © Whitechapel Art Gallery, London

lean against walls or are hung next to the original sketches and ideas in the installation, along with descriptions of journeys, starting-points for pictures and rejected ideas. The images are faintly surreal (a man balancing a plank on his knee, an unlikely bridge between two buildings) and their surrealism is highlighted through the sign-painter's gloss. Medina calls this process 'a collectivity that negotiates its subsistence [through] small scale obstructions, a kind of resistance that operates at the level of *detail*' (Medina 1997: 50).

In his text on walking, Alÿs opens the possibility of continuous in-between in such an action: *as long as* I'm walking; and then he closes it down: I'm *not* choosing. The dialectic between this open and closed position demands a more paradoxical glance at the willed and wilful inhabitant of the field of the in-between (Homi Bhabha's double-visioned migrant?). Refuge and refuse at the same or similar times. Diaspora as absolutely rooted in the paradox of directional pull and its relation to exile.

In the summer of 1997 Alÿs 'walked' the Mexican/American border, echoing the work of Guillermo Gómez-Peña and the Border Arts Workshop:

> I live smack in the fissure between two worlds, in the infected wound: half a block from the end of Western civilisation and four miles from the beginning of the Mexican/American border, the northernmost point of Latin America. In my fractured reality, but a reality nonetheless, there cohabit two histories, languages, cosmologies, artistic traditions, and political systems which are drastically counterposed. Many 'deterritorialised' Latin American artists in Europe and the United States have opted for 'internationalism' (a cultural identity based on the 'most advanced' of the ideas originating out of New York or Paris). I, on the other hand, opt for 'borderness' and assume my role.
>
> (Gómez-Peña 1993: 37)

Paradoxically, walking seems to encompass both 'escape' and 'toil', meanings that are embedded through a meshing of cultural, geographical and class histories, confronted by Alÿs in his *travail* along the border and through the streets of Mexico City (often cited as the ultimate of postmodern cities but demarcated – 'grounded' – before and after theory by pedestrian activity). This walking is, of course, culturally marked although often invisible below the surface of the city: some walk for leisure, some for protest and others for the purposes of art. Others walk for survival, just as some nomadism is chosen and most diaspora is enforced.

Gordana Stanisic's 1994 installation at the Showroom in London elaborates very simply on some of the themes at issue in the work of Vallet Kleiner, Yassour and Alÿs. A student in London, unable to return to her home city of Belgrade because of the very real problem of border crossing and ethnic division within her 'previous territory', Stanisic simply walked the amount of miles back to Belgrade on the type of walking machine used in the fitness industry. Each evening, at the end of a day's constant activity, the artist drew her progress on to a map of Europe on the gallery wall. This quiet testimony to the map, the migrant and the

• *Installation*, Gordana Stanisic, the Showroom, London, 1996. Photo: Hugo Glendinning

experience of diaspora, engaged as it was with the emotional pull of 'homeland', presented a troubled representation of the difficult endurance of the coerced nomad.

> An unruly crowd of descriptive/interpretive terms now jostle and converse in an effort to characterise the contact zones of nations, cultures and regions: terms such as 'border', 'travel', 'creolisation', 'transculturation', 'hybridity' and 'diaspora' (as well as the looser 'diasporic').
> (Clifford 1997: 245)

Clifford points out the violence of the loss of specificity involved in the smooth space of the 'field' (which, both in anthropological terms and in those of recurrent contemporary metaphors, is as likely to be a city as it is a rural clearing). This violence is evoked through the loss of a path, the loss of a boundary, the loss of a recognizable node on the landscape, particularly when those marks of precision and recognition have been destroyed by either fieldworkers or co-opted inhabitants of the field. But the loss of the local and the particular is marked in the step of the walker *at the same time* as his or her movement into the future.*

What would it mean to consider the postmodern as a refuge – an all-inclusive site that is both easily accessible and unnameable? Such impossible inclusivity is on offer in contemporary examples, from the over-use of the term 'performativity' to describe anything that moves (position, place, gender, geography) through to neo-fluxus improvisations, the popular and sexualized 'anything goes' and the partially available 'freedom' of cyberspace.

The marked shift towards expanded definitions of geography, architecture, anthropology and art

* The work in Britain of theatre directors such as Graeme Miller, Chris Heighes and Ewan Forster is an important attempt to reintegrate ideas of local history and pedestrian experience into contemporary performance practice.

(which has been aided by the destabilizing theories of feminism, psychoanalysis and post-colonialism) reflects a philosophical movement from the dualism of the modern towards a constantly reconfigured 'in-between'. A simple marker of this move can be seen in the popularity of the terminologies of ambivalence inherited from Freud, those of Heidegger's 'becoming', the gender questioning from de Beauvoir to Haraway and the insistence on dislocation in Bhabha or Soja. In this new gap (or 'space') – and often with complex results – there is a move to create a discursive set of operations and ambiguous subjectivities. The rejoinder in (the wake of) modernist arts discourse comes in the form of the troubled object, the pedestrian action and its relation to everyday life; the 'space' of 'difference' that eschews production in favour of the negotiated, the future-imaginary, the *difficulty* of translation.

• *Istanbul–Helsinki (La Traversée du Vide)*, Vallet Kleiner, 1997. Videoprint: D. Vallet Kleiner

Is it possible to inhabit the passage (with all its ambivalent references) but to do so in an interrogative fashion? A fashion that reclaims the passage as a place of resistance rather than a place of refuge? Or is the place of refuge a useful one, in which important work gets done – incomplete work in the in-between whose freedom is boundless? The coerced traveller may find no refuge but might adopt clever and intricate forms of social and psychological resistance to counteract difficult terrains; this can be seen in Bhabha's idea of 'sly civility' (Bhabha 1994) or de Certeau's invocation of 'making do' (de Certeau 1984). Benjamin's naming of the passage as the place in which such activity might occur has been dissipated by the attention postmodernity has given to the space of quiescent liberation. It would seem to me that this passage – this place of transient, evasive movement out of the problematic of architecture and into the free spatial and temporal zone – is becoming less a place of resistance and more a refuge from the critical and physical demands of translation.

REFERENCES

Benjamin, Walter (1979) *One Way Street and Other Writings*, London: Verso.

Bhabha, Homi (1994) *The Location of Culture*, London: Routledge.

Clifford, James (1997) *Routes: Travel and Translation in the Late Twentieth Century*, Cambridge, MA: Harvard University Press.

de Certeau, Michel (1984) *The Practice of Everyday Life*, Los Angeles: University of California Press.

Deleuze, Gilles and Guattari, Félix (1988) 'Treatise on Nomadology' in *A Thousand Plateaus: Capitalism and Schizophrenia*, London: Athlone.

Fried, Michael (1967) 'Art and objecthood', *Artforum* 2(2) (June).

Gómez-Peña, Guillermo (1993) *Warrior for Gringostroika*, St Paul, MN: Graywolf Press.

Krauss, Rosalind (1977) *Passages in Modern Sculpture*, London: Viking.

Medina, Cuauhtenoc (1997) 'Francis Alys: Tu subrealismo (Your subrealism)', *Third Text* 38 (Spring): 39–54, London: Kala Press.

Photogrammetry

medium shot of a highly constructed refuge

desperate optimists present a hypothetical story about photogrammetry, fortune-tellers, dance music and their own personal experience of geographical and cultural displacement. There is one character, *Nora*. She is both compulsive and restless but more than that she has a condition known in the medical field as *Blarney's Syndrome* - a disorder causing the patient to make momentary digressions (usually triggered by a word or a fleeting image) from the real world around them. The patient gets obsessively stuck on an idea or a memory and can often appear rapt in thought oblivious to everything going on around them. Until the attack passes the sufferer is rendered totally incapable of doing anything productive or meaningful. This 'condition' is understood to be found almost exclusively among people susceptible to pre-millennial tension. Nora's story begins here - somewhere in Europe - in your typical (aspirational) living room.

Blarney stone
Built into the southern wall of Blarney Castle, in County Cork, Ireland, the Blarney stone is supposed to endow those who kiss it with the gift of eloquence. According to legend, the castle was once saved from attack through flattery and cajolery; hence, the power of the stone, and the word blarney itself.

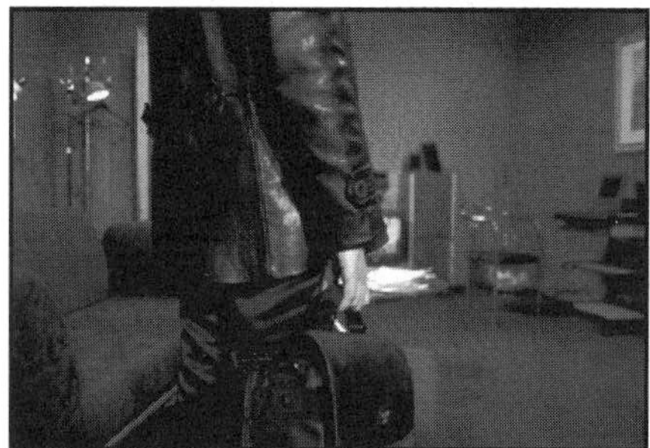

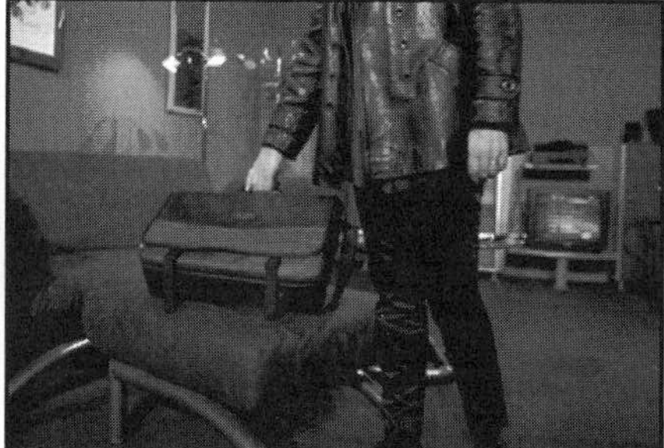

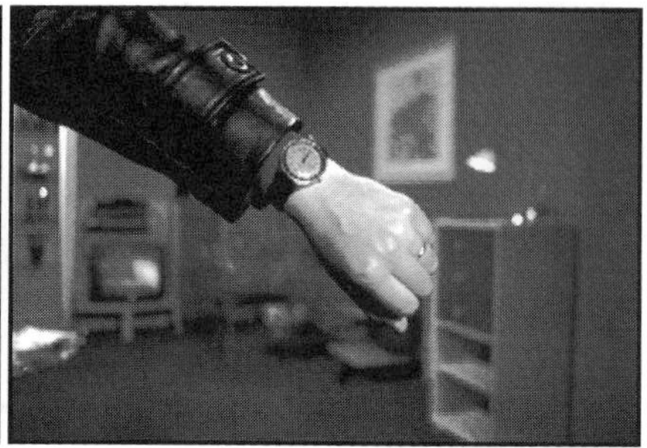

It is night. Nora returns back from somewhere. It's not clear from where. Perhaps it doesn't matter. What matters is that she's back. She checks her watch and sees that it's late. "Could it really be that late?", she asks herself. She begins to think about the day. Her mind drifts back to the morning when she met someone - a stranger. She remembers his big hands. Extra big. She remembers he described himself as an 'inland navigator', before laughing. Loud.

Outline of conversation between Nora and the stranger

The conversation takes place on a bus or maybe even a train. The important point is that the conversation takes place 'in transit'. He is older than her and she is very agitated. Her agitation makes him feel uncomfortable but yet he is unable to leave - partly because it's not his stop, partly because she has him hemmed in and partly because he finds himself compelled to listen to her. She talks directly at him for a long time about her desire - no, her need - to see things from a great height. She tells him about the first time she ever saw a satellite picture of the earth and how that had made her cry. She talks about how happy she feels when she is in an aeroplane looking down at the landscapes and cityscapes below. She talks about the happiness she feels when she's in between two places - when she's nowhere really. She talks very slowly and deliberately (easing up on the eye-to-eye contact) about the experience of being on top of a very tall building. She explains that that is why she loves cities. Big cities. In particular she's thinking about New York. She says, hand on heart, "That is why they built New York that way." It was built for people like her. For people who get giddy. People who have a need to escape. She spins out a long integrated theory about the relationship between cities, emigration, nomadism, desire, displacement and vertigo. The theory takes exactly 12 stops to explain. At this point the man on the bus/train has long ago missed his stop but he still manages to laugh to himself thinking about his long forgotten childhood fascination with homing pigeons and how he had always loved his birds. He had always wanted to know if they read the landscape below like a map. That's when he first became interested in roads, veins and arteries on the surface exposed - criss-crossing the landscape, taking you away but also bringing you back.

Navvy
An abbreviation of *navigator*. A navvy is employed in excavating for roads, railways and canals.
Pigeon racing
Pigeon racing is the sport of racing selectively bred homing pigeons over various long distances. During the first week of the summer racing season, races are about 160 km (100 mi) long. With each successive week the distances increase until a race may be as long as 800-965 km (500-600 mi). Birds that compete in races of 1,450 km (900 mi) or longer are usually older and these races cannot be completed during a single day (pigeons do not fly at night). The winning pigeon returns to its home loft faster than its competitors.

She makes herself comfortable and puts on the TV. She flicks through the stations. She asks herself, "Where would I be without extra-terrestrial television?" Something on channel 34 catches her attention. She watches and listens. Something terrible has happened and the police (and the media) are focusing their attention on a field. The atmosphere is tense and there is much speculation.

Outline of Nora's thoughts regarding a childhood refuge

Nora thinks of a place: a collection of fields at the back of a housing estate in Finglas, Dublin. These fields were known to all the kids in the area as the blackberry fields (or the 'blacker' for short). All the children would play there. The fields were big. They seemed endless. The fields were both exciting and terrifying. Gangs of kids would go to the fields because it was the *best* place. Mathematics, for some reason, seemed important - each field being carefully numbered. Field number one was the field you entered first. Field number two was the next field and so on. The higher the number the deeper into the unknown you went. The deeper you ventured the more your sense of excitement grew and by the same token your sense of terror. Also, the deeper into the fields you went the stranger it felt. Weird things could happen, the worst and the best was to be expected. It was known to everyone that somewhere very very very deep into the numbers, definitely beyond 6 possibly 8 perhaps even beyond 10 or 11, lived the man who owned the blackberry fields. He had a name too: Melvin. Melvin was to be feared. It was impossible to imagine the damage he would do to any unfortunate child caught on his property. Recalling the sense of panic she would feel even on hearing the name Melvin reminded Nora that being in the fields was not an entirely comfortable experience - you didn't go there to take it easy. After all, the fields weren't part of the everyday. You went there to get away from the familiar, the mundane, the expected. The adults went to the pub - the kids went to the blackberry fields. She thinks about a special feature of the fields and Melvin. Because of the close proximity of the housing estate to Dublin Airport the noisy, constant presence of aeroplanes had to be accounted for and explained away by the kids. Therefore, it was an established belief that Melvin owned all the planes and, on a daily basis, he would survey his land, partly to find children to punish and partly to spy on their secret, private world where adventures were had, horrors were witnessed, cruelty was rampant, rules were broken and a strange mixture of freedom and danger seemed always present. Nora thinks now about Melvin in his plane. She always longed to be caught by Melvin and she secretly felt that she could withstand any hideous torture meted out by him in exchange for a view of her world from up there in the clouds.

Nadar
Nadar, the pseudonym of Frenchman Gaspard Felix Tournachon, b. 6 April 1820, d. 15 Mar. 1910, won fame as a journalist, caricaturist, and portrait photographer and was also one of the liveliest personalities of Second Empire Paris. Nadar's reputation as a spirited iconoclast was enhanced by his exploits in his enormous balloon, Le Géant. He made the world's first aerial photographs (1858) from this balloon.

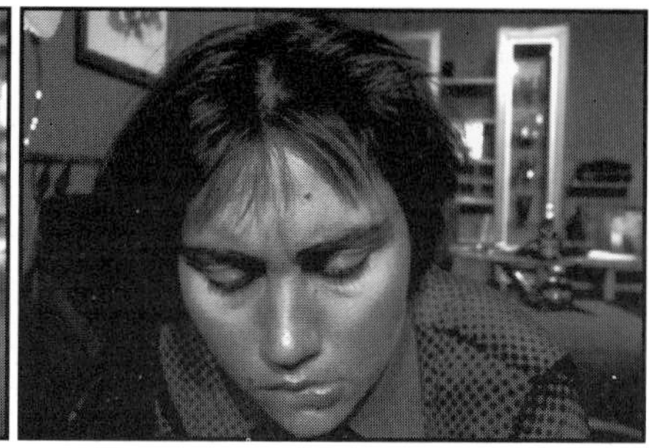

Nora has this sudden need to talk to a friend from home. She phones someone. They're not in. So, she goes through all the names in her telephone book until finally, she gets through to someone named Sean. For the next ten minutes Sean has to listen to this person, whom he hasn't seen for years, go on and on about some fields in a part of Dublin he has never even visited.

Outline of telephone call detailing possible anecdotes

This was the place where some children saw their very first dirty picture. No one said who owned it - it was just 'found'. No matter, they all looked at it in silence for ages and ages.

This is the place where Dessy Ryan picked up a bunch of nettles, grabbed Joseph McGuinness, pulled his pants down and whipped him across the backside. Dessy laughed. Joe lay crying and bleeding. Everyone else just watched.

This is the spot where J. P. Molloy was chased down by 12 Teddyboys. They stood in a big ring around him and ordered him to take his pants down so as they could have a good look. The gang of showaddywaddy lookalikes stood laughing for ages as the half clothed, petrified boy promised them all great wealth IF they'd let him go!

Beyond this point only certain children would venture. These children were different - possibly weird, possibly special.

This is exactly where Sharon Kavanagh stood the day she said, with tears running down her face, that she was glad she was in the fields and not at home with her father.

It was precisely here Emer Kennedy stood and shouted, "I'm never going to die." She was only 8.

This is the place where Gillian Doyle ate loads of unwashed blackberries and then got worms. This happened often!

This is where a group of children got drunk on a naggen of vodka. They lay on their backs and looked up. Some watched the planes go by, and some watched the mountains in the distance, and Alison Flood swore blind that she saw the face of the devil in a cloud.

This is where a cat was drowned by accident.

This is the place where kids set part of a field on fire and it looked brilliant! They all stood watching with big smiles on their faces.

It was approximately here that Richie Flanagan showed everyone his arse. The next week he showed a few people his pubic hair. The week after that there was much talk about him showing his erection to someone.

This was the spot where everyone played the competition, 'who can put up with the most pain'.

It was just beyond this spot that four children watched their friend, Christopher Kelly, get electrocuted on a pylon. Chris went on fire and died. This was the last time all those kids played in the fields. They stopped, not because they were told to but because they found they weren't interested any more.

This is the spot where Anthony Powell jumped from a tree and broke his leg. All the other children could see the bone sticking out. Everyone, including Anthony, looked in silence at the mess for what seemed an eternity.

Everyone learnt to smoke here. The favourite brand was Pall Mall. Some kids even inhaled!

This is where loads of kids saw a horse trapped in a ditch with barbed wire wrapped around its neck.

Suburbs

A suburb is an outlying community that is usually socially and economically linked to a nearby CITY. Suburbs are characteristically located beyond the city limits. Suburbs depend on rapid, flexible modes of transportation and communication, especially the automobile, truck, and telephone. Suburban residents, on the average, have higher incomes than city dwellers and are better educated. Besides the well-known middle-class suburbs, however, there are suburban slums, and suburbs inhabited mainly by the elderly or by particular racial and ethnic groups.

All this talk about the fields makes Nora homesick. She doesn't like this feeling when it comes upon her and so she starts to drink. She looks around the room for distractions. She finally goes to the hi-fi and puts on some music. She can't decide if she should put on dj Shadow or Shara Nelson or Tricky or Funky Porcini or Ice-T or Space or Depth Charge or Daniel O'Donnell. She eventually puts on, Now That's What I Call Music '97. She stands in the middle of the room. Her feelings about this room are ambivalent. She has no commitment to this place. She knows that some time in the near future she will be on the move again. She lists all the objects in the room that belong to her. She looks at each object in turn and then names it out loud. She has this deep sense of not belonging anywhere any more. Sometimes this makes her sad but mostly she accepts it as a condition of the life that she has constructed for herself. She remembers a bad day not so long ago when she was feeling particularly adrift. That day she went to a gypsy fortune-teller. It seemed, at the time, a logical thing to do. She holds her right hand out in front of her. This hand has always appeared larger than life since that day when the fortune-teller ran her finger across the surface of its skin and made this hand a site of images and truths and predictions and traumas. There was no escaping this hand. No escaping the life mapped out in its lines and crevices. The fortune-teller had looked straight into her eyes and said, "I see both good and bad news here. Are you sure you want to hear everything I have to say? I can stop now and give you your money back but if you stay you will have to listen to everything."

She stayed.

The fortune-teller told her, at great length, many things but the one thing that occupied her thoughts the most was the prediction that she will always feel a sense of loss in her life - not anything she could clearly articulate or put her finger on but a sense of loss all the same. A sense that things will never feel complete. This sense, she was told, will keep her on the move and keep her looking. However, the fortune-teller was adamant on this particular point without ever explaining why, that the process of searching for something which ultimately could never be found would be a worthwhile one. Her attention is suddenly distracted because her favourite song of the moment is playing. She goes over to the c.d. and whacks up the volume.

Outline of Nora's favourite track

The song, Free, is by Ultra Naté. It was the hugely successful summer hit of 1997 that was played in all the popular resorts including Ibiza, Malaga and Majorca. The lyrics are upbeat and catchy, "Cause you're freeeee to be what you want to beeeee.....". Nora likes songs with a good, positive message. In the summer. The winter is different. In the winter she will only listen to songs that remind her of home.

Gypsies
Although mingled with other populations, the Gypsies are a distinct ethnic group that originated in north central India. At the time of their first migrations into Europe these landless wanderers earned their living as entertainers, magicians, blacksmiths, and horse dealers. They rejected settled occupations. The Roman Catholic Church forbade association with Gypsy fortune-tellers. The Gypsies' unwillingness to settle, assimilate, and become Christian made them targets for persecution. They prefer to be self-employed. The most common occupation for the women is fortune-telling, usually by palmistry. A common occupation for the men is buying and selling used cars and trucks.

Nora dances. Hard. And as she dances she thinks certain thoughts. She doesn't know if these thoughts come from somewhere in between the beats of the music, or from the space of silence that bridges one track to the next, or perhaps from the evocative lyrics, or maybe from the subliminal messages hidden in the TV that's going on in the background. Regardless of their source, they are there and they won't go away and she can't fully understand them yet she recognises them as being somehow important and central to her life. All these blurred images seem to map out places which she has, at one time or other, referred to as 'home' but there is this one image, one image more strange and persistent than the rest...

Outline of Nora's one persistent image

Storage unit
A storage unit is a place where people store their belongings. Often these people are homeless. Often these units take the form of large wooden crates with words like 'Pickfords' stamped on the side but occasionally they can be strange, eerie, magical places - long, shiny, endless corridors with each unit carefully and individually numbered, e.g. 4B10. These units vary in size and shape. Competitive London prices are as follows: 20 sq. ft. @ £39.00 per month; 40 sq. ft. @ £65.00 per month; 60 sq. ft. @ £90.00 per month; 80 sq. ft. @ £110.00 per month and so on. The trading terms normally specify one month's rent in advance and one month's rent to act as a deposit.

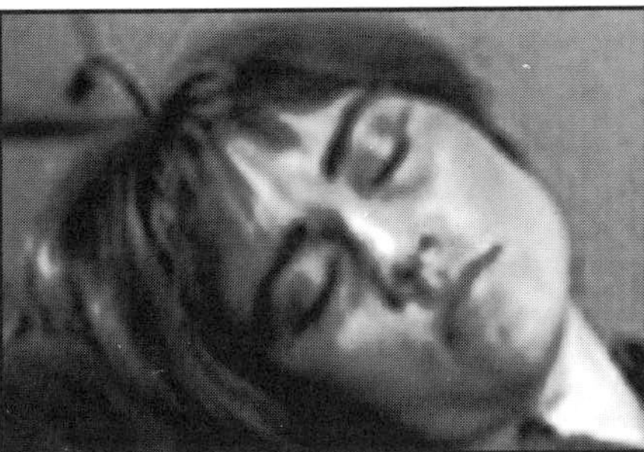

After the dancing Nora sleeps. Deep. And she dreams. This is no ordinary dream - it is a photogrammetric dream. The kind of dream that only a vicious combination of dancing, alcohol, fatigue and a sense of dislocation can produce.

Outline of Nora's photogrammetric dream

Nora gets glimpses of maps. Being photogrammetric maps, these maps are both technical and highly informative. This is lucky really because what she needs, more than anything else in her life right now, is a vision of things which is uncomplicated by either subjectivity or that certain anxiety dreaming can often produce. During this protracted dream she surveys many landscapes and cities and suburban dwellings and as she does so she begins to recite, like a prayer, a question, "Could I live there?" In answering this question she lays down a set of preconditions which make a series of demands upon each particular place:

only if I could get a roof over my head there
only if I could dream there
only if I could be warm there
only if it brought out the best in me
only if I could be safe there
only if I could be happy there
only if it was a good place
only if I could eat there
only if I could find love there
only if I could make mistakes there
only if I could get a job there
only if there were tall buildings there
only If I could cry there
only if I could die with dignity there
only if I could laugh there
only if I could fuck and fuck and fuck there
only if I could pretend there
only if the days were generally longer than the nights
only if I could speak my mind there
only if I could scream there
only if there were plenty of opportunities to let my hair down
only if I could distinguish between what has value and what has not
only if I could be productive there
only if I wasn't scared there
only if I could think there

Photogrammetry
Photogrammetry is the science or art of obtaining reliable measurements and/or preparing maps and charts from aerial photographs using stereoscopic equipment and methods. Aerial photography (using the balloon as a platform in the 19th century and, after 1910, the airplane) revolutionised mapping to as great an extent as did printing in the Renaissance or the use of satellites and the computer in the second half of the 20th century.

wide shot of a highly constructed refuge

And the list goes on like this. And this list seems hopelessly doomed because it's clear, even to her, that if she continues to make such demands upon the world she'll never find what she is searching for. Finally, she sees a feature on a map. At first she isn't certain exactly what she is looking at. Then she recognises it for what it is. She sees an image of herself sitting on a chair in a living room. It's apparent though that this is not her living room, instead it's a product of her imagination. An imagination that is prepared to try any cheap tactic to locate her in a 'home'.

Finally
No more footnotes. Nothing else to be said.

Performing Displacement: desperate optimists and the Arts of Impropriety

Andrew Quick

I am sitting at a table and I am looking at a map. How do things look on this map? Very clear and peaceful, and uncomplicated. I can't see any signs of life – no traces of human suffering – just a surface, showing outlines of different places. What am I thinking? I am thinking that this is wonderful and I point with my finger to a place on this map (any place, it doesn't matter where!) and I say, 'See this place, doesn't it look good? I want to live there. Tell me, what do I have to do to get there? I am prepared to do anything'.

(desperate optimists 1993: 2)

To walk is to lack a place.

(de Certeau 1984: 103)

A refuge is a place of safety or security; a shelter, an asylum. Most of all, a refuge is a stronghold. Refugees are people in need of such a place. Displaced, they seek protection, a new home, or at least a 'good' place in which to wait before returning to their landscapes of origin. Perhaps, the theatre is also a place of refuge; a place in which the various participants of performance seek some sort of solace, some sort of comfort; a site in which they might identify who and what they are. After all why do we keep being drawn to something that often appears to be so absurd: the practice of making a pretence of reality or of making a reality of pretence in a cave of shadows. For surely, despite Plato's admonishment of what he presumed were arts of illusion, theatre's flickerings intimate origins, of being something, somewhere, in the world.

In his extraordinary book *The Practice of Everyday Life*, Michel de Certeau reminds us time and time again that place and the mechanisms of its creation inaugurate identity; that the institutions of knowledge and power operate through placing to create the individual, the city and the state (de Certeau 1984). These institutions, he points out, always seek to confine and control and establish the 'proper' – the basis of the autonomous place. The proper, de Certeau argues, is 'a mastery of places through sight'. This marking-out of space, this capacity to divide and re-order, is a panoptic practice which, he tells us, 'proceeds from a place whence the eye can transform foreign forces and objects that can be observed and measured' (de Certeau 1984: 36). Those forces and bodies that resist the strategic operations of place are either consumed by the proper or forced to flee, to become homeless entities waiting for the moment when they might reassert their autonomy, establish their own place, their own ground (*topos*) in which to 'properly' be. The dynamics that create the autonomous place either consume everything other

Performance Research 2(3), pp.25-29 © Routledge 1997

than it or force another autonomous place (individual, community, city, state) to exist in separation or stand in opposition. This is the contradiction inherent within a politics of place and is, perhaps, why we should always question our investment in its formation.*

* For an excellent analysis of the desire for security and certitude see Dillon 1997.

I have asserted in other writings that the theatre, as an institution, is a proper place which, through its mechanisms, attempts to master time and the body; a place which attempts to appropriate everything external to its limits within its internal dynamics.† To summarize, the theatre operates as a spatial machine, a representational apparatus, that asserts a mastery over everything that exists beyond its limits through the process of incorporation. The theatre bends to its rules everything it attempts to present and re-creates its 'outside' according to its representational principles. The 'exterior to the theatre' limit, what might be called 'the real', is transformed into the object for this appropriation. Put another way, the theatre makes 'sense' of the real by transforming it into signs. This operation also has the effect of turning the exterior into that which is re-presented in the interior space. Of course, many practitioners (Grotowski is the most obvious example) have sought to escape this process of representation by taking flight from the theatre space only to find that its dynamics follow or haunt their attempted presentations in 'the real world' (in Grotowski's case in monastic dedication, in the forest – in 'nature').

† See Quick (1994) and (1997).

Is it possible, then, to create a 'nowhere', a 'no-place'; to establish a utopia (literally: no place, from the Greek *ou*, 'not' + *topos*, 'a place'); 'a place' which is resistant to the incorporating operations of representation? After all, as Oscar Wilde reminds us, a map without Utopia drawn upon it is not worth having. The invocation of an alternative to the boundaries of the map, to the limits of representation, will always itself be bounded by the idealism of imagination. Moreover, even the utopian assertion of place will operate through the same exclusionary logics: the establishment of difference, of separation or of violent assimilation. As with the work of Impact Theatre and Forced Entertainment, desperate optimists are engaged in an aesthetics of performance which seeks to present both the desire and the failure to attain a utopia, a better place, a place beyond the limits of the theatrical-representational machine. While always prone to a process of disappearance such places momentarily configure when certain practices destabilize and open out the authoritarian rule of representation. This is not to say that these practices exist *per se* in an experimental tradition of theatre-making (although they ghost in most theatrical traditions) but rather that particular practitioners create performances that form (and disappear) through a working-through of the dynamics of destabilization: a working-through which wears away at the mechanisms of theatricality itself. *Inside* the place of theatre, like refugees, these practitioners remain strangers – 'outsiders' – always somewhat 'foreign' to its mechanisms, existing within, and yet always apart from, its limit-defining systems.

The performance work of Christine Molloy and Jo Lawlor, the core members of desperate optimists, appears to be that of such internal outsiders. As they are practitioners from Dublin who have primarily made and performed work in Britain and mainland Europe, this identification has another resonance, one that is always haunted by the histories of oppression and colonization that shore up Britain's relationship to its neighbouring island. From Britain the readership of this work is inevitably framed through specific perceptions of 'Irishness', more or less romantic, involving narratives and mythologies of nationhood in which the figures of the immigrant and the exiled are prominent. Whilst these elements cannot be ignored in relationship to the work of desperate optimists, indeed some of them are directly referenced in their performances, I think it is important not to reduce their practices of displacement to a reading limited by the politics of nation. This is not to lessen the relevance of their Irish origins or to ignore the fact that they have migrated from their homeland, but to argue that their work negotiates notions of space, narrative, home as sanctuary, and the hope of (re)discovering a secure landscape, *beyond* metaphors of nationhood. I would like to argue that, through their use of particular practices within the theatre space itself, this work *puts into question the very mechanisms that construct notions of identity and origin;* how, through their experimentation with theatrical form, they open out the confining limits of representation and articulate a broad politics in the arts of dis-placement.

In *Anatomy of Two Exiles*, first performed in 1992, narratives of national and individual identity are directly addressed as Molloy and Lawlor attempt to articulate personal histories, symbolic objects and cultural artefacts in a coherent version/vision of an originary place. The performance is constructed through a mixture of direct address to the audience and dialogue between the two people on the stage who speak and wander about the playing space 'without' the conventional theatrical framework of sustained fictional characterization. Here the performers present 'themselves', constructing a performance through confession, through story-telling, through minor disagreements, through the endeavour to link disparate phrases and artefacts into an impossible whole. This piece's multiple narratives relate directly to the artist's personal experiences and seem to cohere most powerfully around memories of childhood, a mother's emigration to America, and the thematic of exile from a homeland. The tone is conversational and the performed actions are undertaken in a relaxed and unhurried manner. Records are played, tapes are listened to, statements are made, Polaroids are taken, a scene from a play is attempted and dialogues are engaged with in the endeavour to retrieve for themselves, and for the audience, a lost landscape of origin. Objects litter the floor of the playing space: stones, potatoes, clods of earth, building bricks, a statue of the Virgin Mary, a miniature Statue of Liberty, a model of a white stone cottage. As each performer engages with these items in the quest to uncover and discover the structures that might establish and shore up an identity (individual or national), each object begins to assume an iconographic status standing in for and supplementing a unity of self that is evidently already lost.

• *Anatomy of Two Exiles*, 1992. desperate optimists. Photo: Amanda Harman

As I have indicated, the autonomous place necessary to identity has to be constructed through an operation, a performance, that is always masterful; a performance in which narratives and objects are ordered into hierarchical systems that coalesce to form an untroubled history, an untroubled account of the individual and the national. It is important that the representational machine not only runs smoothly but also conceals the very mechanisms that allow it to operate. In *Anatomy of Two Exiles*, however, performance is revealed to be forever failing. Here, fragments of narratives are linked through juxtaposition but never construct a complete story. Objects are invested with significance but always seem to fall short of, or remain in excess of, a speculation which promises to mark out a route to an identity. This description of *Anatomy of Two Exiles* might give the impression that the piece is shambolic and unstructured, that the individual performers, appearing to rely on a form of authenticity, lack the skills expected of actors in a more conventional theatre; that as a consequence of working through performed failures the piece in turn fails as a performance. However, despite the clutter of objects that are spread chaotically across the floor by the end of the performance and despite the seemingly evenly paced and pared-down performance style, I am struck by the complex internal structure of the piece and the delicacy of its playing. As I watch the performers negotiate the materials that might construct a map of individual and national identity I am given space and time to locate my own points of contact, to trace out my own trajectories of interaction, to make and lose my own connections. In contrast to the desire for the map, for the security of the known place, the landscape of *Anatomy of Two Exiles* is always on the move, shifting my eye to a periphery in which I am forced, along with its two protagonists, to re-play my own fragile constructions of selfhood.

In *Hope* (1993) the emphasis shifts away from the origin of nationhood as the performers attempt to negotiate the personal place/space of the house and its garden. Home is periodically invoked as a place of security, a place where the loss felt with the restless movement in and of 'the outside' might be arrested or dissipated. In the account of a dream that opens *Hope* the street (the outside) is described as a place of 'danger' and 'hardship' where 'I am forced to keep my head down and just keep moving'. In contrast home is described as a place to dream in and to imagine 'how things might be different' (desperate optimists 1993: 2). As such, the secure home is not just the subject of hope but also the place to construct hope in. As in *Anatomy of Two Exiles*, there is a restless energy to the performance as multiple spaces are set up within the playing area through the movement of lights on stands and the rearrangement of screens. Floor-plans, diagrams indicating possible choreographies and sections of text provide, on stark white panels, a backdrop that constantly shifts the focus of the performance as different and contradictory pieces of information are presented and worked through. Fragments of monologue are sampled and re-mixed on stage creating the sense of a shifting soundscape in which even the security of the spoken word (seemingly authentic, since we heard the word uttered by a body at a particular time and in a specific place) is eroded as it is placed in contexts which are always on the move.

• *Hope*, 1993–4. desperate optimists. Photo: Gill Goddard

Of course, as the performance progresses, the idealization of the house and garden is quickly eroded as the narrative of the Fall in the Garden of Eden is strangely juxtaposed with the conflagration at Wako, Texas, different accounts of childhood memories, and scenes from Alan Ayckbourn's *Absurd Person Singular*. Through this collage the recalled, imagined and idealized refuge becomes as much a site for intrusion, fear, shame, banishment, boredom, imprisonment, abuse and suicide as it does a place of safety. In its constant and varying incarnations the place of home, rather than being fixed and made secure as a representation, seems always to disappear. It is a disappearance that occurs under the weight of attempted rememberings, attempted descriptions and attempted presentations; under the weight of an endless questioning which asks what such a place might be:

> Are you happy to have visitors?
> Are you ashamed of this house?
> Would you say it is a cruel place?
> Would you say it is a warm place?
> Would you say it is a cold place?
> Does it bring out the best in you?
> Do you think you deserve better?
> Do you like this house?
>
> (desperate optimists 1993: 10)

The questioning that these performances enact, whether literally here in *Hope* turned towards the notion of home, or in the failed stagings of national identity in *Anatomy of Two Exiles*, or more recently in the unfulfilled quest for a true self in the psychoanalytical tellings of *Indulgence* (1996), thoroughly destabilizes the propriety of place. As practices which put into question notions of place, as performances of displacement, these works are not without value. British performance has all too frequently been framed by the accusation that it is a purely aesthetic practice, a scene without politics. But questions always demand answers. In desperate optimists' putting into question of the formations that construct place I am impelled to reconsider the limitations of the narratives, the histories, the objects and the mechanisms through which a concept of self is constructed, and to reflect not only on the fragility of the performance of my own identity, but also on the possibility that someone, something, always suffers as a consequence of the assertion of the self.*

* I would like to thank Adrian Heathfield for discussions on this piece.

REFERENCES

de Certeau, Michel (1984) *The Practice of Everyday Life*, Berkeley: University of California Press.

desperate optimists (1992) 'Hope', unpublished performance text

Dillon, Michael (1997) *Politics of Security: Towards a Political Philosophy of Continental Thought*, London: Routledge.

Quick, Andrew (1994) 'Searching for angels with cardboard wings: Forced Entertainment and the sublime', *Contemporary Theatre Review*, 2(2):25–35.

Quick, Andrew (1997) 'Troubling practice: opening writing, identity and place', *Shattered Anatomies: Traces of the Body in Performance*, ed. Adrian Heathfield, Bristol: Arnolfini.

Two Continents, No Refuge: Engendering the Problematics of Home

Marcia Blumberg

Refuge denotes a physical place of shelter and a space of safety; for women, especially, it often connotes home since domestic locales may be unproblematically considered synonymous with nurturing environments. David Sibley regards this approach as 'too cosy' since the home

> also provides the context for violence. . . . What is missing from the 'house as haven' thesis is a recognition of the polar tensions surrounding the use of domestic space, tensions which become a part of the problem of domination within families.
>
> (Sibley 1995: 94)

This dynamic is further complicated when circumstances necessitate the inclusion of an outsider in the domestic space. In the 1990 play *A Worm in the Bud* a Victorian spinster seeks refuge from a limiting life in England by devoting herself to a new cause in South Africa but finds herself in the midst of climactic changes and untenable challenges to her deeply held values. Imbued with notions of middle-class Victorian rectitude the governess performs her mission to civilize the Afrikaner family by tutoring the children and attempting to transpose the niceties of British life into rural South Africa. When the new home provides neither well-being nor shelter from her growing but unwelcome desire for her boorish employer, an economy that is apparently fantasized and is, in intellectual terms, antithetical to all she holds dear, the woman develops hysteria and, in a desperate flight from bodily and psychic pain, takes refuge in a self-orchestrated death. My abridged synopsis belies the theatricality and innovative structure of the play by the Afrikaner academic, actor and playwright, Reza de Wet. Written during a period of immense national upheaval, the play evokes what Antonio Gramsci, in another context, has described thus: 'The old is dying and the new cannot be born; in this interregnum there arises a great diversity of morbid symptoms' (Gramsci 1971: 276). During this era of the dismantling of apartheid, the play enacts gender-related issues and the morbid symptomology of home as place and state of mind deploying satirical re-readings of diverse intertexts: a book on Victorian sexuality, *Twelfth Night*, writings of Emily Hobhouse, and poetry. In dramatizing an individual woman's plight in a moribund society weighed down by patriarchal structures and the effects of a deeply disfigured social fabric, the play represents power in a rather monolithic* way; that is, women are constructed chiefly as objects in a patriarchal economy and exhibit only a limited access to agency.

* However, the play as cautionary tale also makes possible readings which foreground a more productive (rather than merely repressive) understanding of power (Foucault 1990: 119). A fuller discussion of productive rather than repressive models of power, specifically with respect to hysterics, is included in a book I am completing, titled 'Engendering intervention in contemporary South African theatre'.

A Worm in the Bud is an ingenious epistolary drama that in performance yokes two writing modes usually gendered female. Letters penned

Performance Research 2(3), pp.30–38 © Routledge 1997

and read by two Victorian ladies – Katy, a married woman and mother, still resident in England, and her sister Emma, a spinster and erstwhile humanitarian, newly arrived in South Africa – are juxtaposed with Emma's diary entries, which transgress the divide between publicly sanctioned mores and private desires. These latter writings form a temporary refuge and are what de Wet calls 'the underbelly of the letters' (Blumberg 1993); they are in effect Emma's letters addressed to herself: 'It's like whispering to myself . . . and listening at the same time' (de Wet 1995: 8). The writings are performed in designated areas of the stage so as to emphasize separations in locale but also to foreground visually the linkage of emotional bonds and societal structures.

Set in 1904 after the Anglo-Boer War, Emma's sojourn with a rural Afrikaner family operates as a site of struggle between Briton and Boer and forms the intersection of discourses of cultural crossings, colonization, gender, race, class and of the problematics of 'home'. Utilizing Una Chaudhuri's term 'geopathology: the problem of place – and place *as* problem' (Chaudhuri 1995: 55) and her argument, in *Staging Place*, that 'who one is and who one can be . . . are a function of *where* one is and how one experiences that place' (ibid.: xii), I investigate the assumption that home is a refuge. Moreover, patriarchal structures and oppressive conditions challenge Chaudhuri's definition of home as 'both shelter and prison, security and entrapment' (ibid.: 8). Emma finds that the negative terms exclude the 'shelter' and 'security' associated with home as refuge.

While de Wet carefully situates her play at the turn of the century by incorporating historical figures and employing appropriate speech patterns and modes of living, she deliberately invokes the present: 'In those days the Afrikaner was the English people's cause. Blacks were regarded as savages. The emphasis has shifted – the impulse remains the same' (Sichel 1990). In addition to the temporal divide the proxemic construction of the play situates the sisters in distant locales, yet Katy is implicated in the events of Emma's life. Similarly the spectators, distanced from the stage space, and apparently historically remote from the events, are provoked neither to feel the 'safety' of these distancings nor to take refuge in a diminished involvement with the sisters' problems.

De Wet's construction of Emma incorporates her own reaction to the impulses the character typifies

> in her way of imposing and thinking that she would save and enlighten the Afrikaner. It was in a way also an analogy for what the liberals were thinking about the black people in Africa. The Afrikaners were a cause for the British. They had a need to impose foreign ideas and 'civilize'. . . . It gave me great joy to see her disintegrating like that.
>
> (quoted in Huismans and Finestone 1995: 95)

In writing this play deeply felt dynamics motivated the playwright, who experienced linguistic and cultural otherness when she moved to the British settler enclave of Grahamstown, where she recalls 'being treated a bit like a savage. I was tolerated as an Afrikaner and regarded very oddly' (Blumberg 1998). Her experience mirrored aspects that she recalled from her grandmother's stories, which came sharply into focus when de Wet read diaries written during forty years: 'She maintained a beautifully harmonious exterior . . . I wasn't aware of her personal sufferings, her doubts and her deep neuroses. She didn't allow them to impinge on us but she expressed them in her diaries' (Blumberg 1998). Over the generations the inability to experience home as a refuge in its extended sense incited the satire: 'A lot of those angers were expressed in the play but filtered through a black comic gothic structure so that it doesn't become didactic or offensive' (Blumberg 1998). While these and other South African narratives no doubt provided material for the play, de Wet was also fascinated by Ronald Pearsall's book, *The Worm in the Bud,* which analysed middle-class Victorian sexual attitudes and evoked the contradictory world from which Emma sought refuge. Dramatizing some of these situations, de Wet exposes the dichotomy between the prohibitions imposed on women and the practices adopted by men. Since marriage was deemed the 'proper' state for women the expectation that they would bear large families not only constituted a health hazard but relegated them to a domestic situation where home could be neither a refuge nor a space of personal growth. In contrast, many husbands of this era idolized their wives and simultaneously averted the 'constrictions' of wedlock by 'enjoying' sex with prostitutes or developing liaisons with mistresses.

A Worm in the Bud also renders problematic the potential of home as a refuge with respect to locale as a physical place and a corporeal space; performance of the silence and simultaneous tumultuous protest of the hysteric's body occurs in Emma's voicing of the hallucinatory transition from severe repression to an intense, terrifying experiencing of sexual desire. Her sense of being possessed by an uncouth and seemingly barbaric Boer is as real to the spinster Emma as her actions appear strange and unsettling to her Afrikaner hosts; so real that it causes psychic disintegration and suicide. The revelation of Emma's death in the opening moments operates as a Brechtian alienation device that refuses suspense and instead frees the audience to concentrate on the unfolding process. Katy's memorial for Emma, a lecture to the Society for the Prevention of Inequality of Women, provides the ostensible occasion for the play. The public lecture and Katy's private letter of loss and perplexity to their father frame the entire staging of the performed epistles and diary entries so that Emma's life is reconstructed in diverse writings that mark the difference between the ventriloquized voicings suitable for public scrutiny and the outpouring of her desires and anarchic conflicts. These supposedly pre-scripted extracts of writing form artificially interrupted and stunted communications. Although this structure eschews conventional dialogue, the performance of letters emphasizes aborted yet desperately sought exchanges especially when stage directions indicate that one woman appears to listen to the other. The play, therefore, renders concrete the sisterly ties through fragments of writing woven together with readings of the women's bodies. Dynamic relations between the overlapping scenes of speech and silence in works and bodies dramatize dis-ease located in one woman but more importantly in society.

De Wet also argues that these relations effect contradictions in the format:

> Private correspondence is also a very refined way of corresponding. I liked that quite delicate framework for the violent impulses that it had to contain. It is such a little Victorian frame and it formed quite a stark contrast to what was actually happening. . . . [A]ll these things were being presented to the father so that he could see how it all happened. It is ultimately the paternal eye that the play is being presented to. And it is that patriarchal eye that has brought about the whole calamity.
>
> (quoted in Huismans and Finestone 1995: 94)

The sisterly eye for which the letters are putatively written and the paternal eye to which they are presented form a structural tension that exemplifies how the genre of letter-writing is subjected to the control of patriarchal structures. These are also imbricated in class and cultural difference so that women who write letters in the play experience the oppressions of patriarchy differently.

A Worm in the Bud also cites and transposes a number of texts. In her satirical re-readings of intertexts and her disruption of anticipated dramatic practice the playwright employs discursive modes which linguistically and thematically approximate and expose structures operating in society at the beginning of the twentieth century, many of which still operate today. Articles and letters by and to Emily Hobhouse as well as other archival materials from the period form an intertextual grid through which de Wet weaves the play.

In writing *A Worm in the Bud* de Wet acknowledges Hobhouse as the inspiration for her character Emma, a satiric re-figuring, who emphasizes complex societal issues both past and present. As Emily and the fictive Emma seem similarly situated at the nexus of gender, marital status and class, so Jennifer Hobhouse Balme's assessment of her great-aunt Emily might well apply to Emma in terms of their philanthropic motivation: 'She could have sat back and led the normal soul-destructive life of a Victorian spinster. But temperamentally she could not, so she gave her life for the benefit of others' (Balme 1994: 593). De Wet effectively recites such turns of phrase and sentiments of the time as that found in Jan Hofmeyer's letter to Emily of 10 July 1901: 'you have let a ray of light and hope into many depressed and desperate hearts' (quoted in Balme 1994: 250). Her adoption of specific linguistic modes in English constitutes an intervention for this Afrikaans playwright:

> The irony of it pleased me immensely. I used the [colonizers'] language to launch an attack on the colonial attitude. I had become very irritated by the colonial way of looking at the Afrikaners here in Grahamstown.
> (quoted in Huismans and Finestone 1995: 94)

While satire provides the vehicle for de Wet's attack she also relishes the opportunity to write from an oppositional perspective. In the play, Emma's stated mission – 'My calling is a noble one – to foster greater understanding between our two nations. I can already imagine . . . enlightenment dawning on the sea of upturned faces' (de Wet 1995: 8) – replicates the Hobhousian prose. It also stresses Emma's unexamined premises and reeks of the condescension that she exudes throughout the play. The playwright analyses this posture:

> I've always been interested in the need to uplift and educate and in the assumption that the things that are intrinsically part of another culture are backward or uncivilised. . . . It reflects a real fear of the other.
> (quoted in Wren 1990: 21)

Here de Wet refers to the setting of the play and the particular impulse that propelled some of the British to attempt to 'civilize' the Boers. Her conviction about the replication of this dynamic in contemporary South Africa emphasizes the parallels for local spectators. Although specific allusions might be lost if this play were to be produced in another country, Emma's sense of superiority, embedded so markedly in racial and class structures, certainly obtains in other cultures as does a gender hierarchy that operates in complex ways to devalorize women. The shared racial grouping of Emma and her employer, Mr Brand, is one factor of supposed equality; she is, however, upper middle class and considers him beneath her, yet, at the same time, the hierarchy of gender elevates him to a position of authority. This intricate network of relationships exemplifies Chandra Talpede Mohanty's argument about the 'complex *relationality* that shapes our social and political lives' (Mohanty 1991: 13).

Emma assumes that England is the epitome of civilization and that its culture, conventions and social mores are models of excellence that should be emulated by all; this stance is evident throughout the play, perhaps most pointedly in her musings under the rubric 'The typical Boer'. In her categorization of the 'authentic Boer in his natural habitat' (de Wet 1995: 4), Emma occupies the position of a supposedly objective observer recording scientific data. Her epithets and value judgements soon, however, betray her disdain for the subjects of her inquiry, 'half-civilized people who are too thickheaded to know they are standing in the path of that Juggernaut, progress' (ibid.: 4), and recall other statements by Victorian Englishmen and Englishwomen, such as 'the greatest enemy of the Boer woman was the Boer woman herself with her ignorance, filth, insanitary habits and immoral crowding' (quoted in Hewison 1980: 196). In direct contrast to Emily's support of the Boer women and their handling of what she regards as an untenable situation, Emma's distaste for the Boers' uncouthness, superstition, folk remedies and adherence to the Bible, widespread illiteracy and lack of interest in culture, betrays her own rigidity and anticipates the return of what she has seemingly so well repressed.

The *mise-en-scène* of *A Worm in the Bud* foregrounds the elevated notions of British civilization and the material effects of its enactment. The locale of the married sister, Katy, is a '*small "upper" area . . . a miniature version of the Victorian "gilded cage". There is a claustrophobic profusion of ferns and palms, a small Victorian table and chair, and an armchair'* (de Wet 1995: 2). This small crowded area visually highlights Katy's multiple entrapment and its placement at the upper level stresses the greater value and power of anything British since such proxemics places Katy in a position where she literally speaks down to the audience and to Emma in her sparse South African setting. Katy's spatial confinement also underscores the restrictions of the rigid codes of Victorian behaviour especially in her embodiment as a fragile ever-pregnant woman now awaiting the birth of her fourth child and fully cognizant of previous protracted births, where 'forceps were applied but I expected no less since we women were made to suffer' (ibid.: 9). Her doctor's answer to recurrent bouts of illness is revealing: 'The female functions must be controlled . . . or there is no telling what else may be wrong!' (de Wet 1995: 11). Strictures of the female body also signify the extreme repression of female sexuality, which, as we focus on the unfolding performance of Emma's story, anticipates her 'condition'. On the one hand this position as an hysteric apparently epitomizes her inability to feel at home and seek refuge of a kind in her own corporeal space; on the other hand it embodies the voicing of unacknowledged and long-silenced desires.

Control of the female body as a sign of the controls and strictures of their lives foregrounds the relegation of many Victorian women to the status of 'angel in the house', which Nina Auerbach reminds us is 'a violent paradox with overtones of benediction and captivity' (Auerbach 1982: 72). Katy's unquestioned acceptance of marriage with its concomitant physical and psychological toll of multiple pregnancies and high child mortality and her genteel comments on the inevitability of a woman's fate actualize one image of Victorian women. Martha Vicinus also focuses attention on the married woman: 'the cornerstone of Victorian society was the family; the perfect lady's sole function was marriage and procreation (the two, needless to say were considered as one)' (Vicinus 1973: x); by juxtaposing marriage as a normative state and spinsterhood as a societal blunder, Vicinus asks, 'What of those who failed to marry? . . . Only the exceptionally fortunate and courageous might succeed through emigration. . . . All social forces combined to leave the spinster emotionally and financially bankrupt' (Vicinus 1973: x, xii). Pearsall discerns one exception: 'Being a governess was second best to being married. . . . [it] was a position girls of good breeding could hold without shame.' (Pearsall 1993: 262). Michelle Adler is less optimistic when she terms the position of governess 'the last resort for respectable women' in straitened circumstances (Adler 1996: 87). Furthermore, Auerbach cautions about

> the common ambiguous social situation old maid and fallen woman shared. Not only did both exist amorphously beyond women's traditional identities as daughter, wife, and mother, but both were associated with exile in all its resonant confusion between criminal degradation and missionary heroism.
>
> (Auerbach 1982: 153)

While Emma purportedly takes refuge in South Africa as a governess she is both an exile from England in terms of a satirized missionary heroism and an exile from self-knowledge seemingly plunged into a state of degradation.

Intertextual resonances in the play also emphasize other voicings that relate the gender-stereotypical behaviour and expectations in Victorian England to an inability to feel at home within clearly defined roles. In the opening and closing moments of the play two young girls sing an untitled song; this, constituting the first four lines of Robert Louis Stevenson's poem 'A Good Boy', ironically highlights gender difference by emphasizing the desire for girls to emulate the practices and measure up to the standards of boys.

Twelfth Night provides the significant titular citation for de Wet's play as it did for Pearsall's book. De Wet's *A Worm in the Bud* and Shakespeare's *Twelfth Night* dramatize sea voyages to new worlds as common plot initiators and foreground the reading and interpretation of letters. In constructing her miniature stagescape, de Wet chooses from the diverse cast of Shakespearean characters to spotlight Viola and an imagined sister. The shipwrecked Viola's survival strategy includes taking refuge in impersonating the male page Cesario, who offers 'his' services to Duke Orsino. Viola's self-reflexive stance is evident in dialogue with Olivia, the object of Orsino's desire: 'I am not that I play' (I.v.185), and later with the Duke, 'I am not what I am' (III.i.43). As Cesario, Viola admits that she might love her employer if she were a woman like her love-lorn sister, whose history, she informs him, was

> A blank, my lord: she never told her love,
> But let concealment like a worm i' th' bud
> Feed on her damask cheek; she pin'd in thought
> And with a green and yellow melancholy
> She sat like Patience on a monument,
> Smiling at grief.
>
> (II.iv.110–16)

De Wet's satire renders material the blank in her construction of two sisters; Katy, moreover, frames the narration to preclude her sister's history from becoming an empty signifier or a tarnished text woven together by rumour and maliciousness.

Instead, Katy presents a memorial tribute, which embodies Emma's public voice in letters and the private tortuous conflicts of her diary entries. This re-writing of the Shakespearean text points to such comparable issues as Viola's ventriloquizing of an invented sister and the re-presentation of Emma's voice performed partially by Katy but also corporeally realized in the appearance of the now deceased Emma as she voices her anguish. Barbara Freedman aptly reminds us that Viola's 'physical disguise is only one aspect of her awareness that identity is a function of self-alienation . . . consider at how many removes Viola speaks . . . she chooses to hide behind the role of the masked and unacknowledged lover' (Freedman 1991: 218–19). If Viola knowingly hides behind the mask, Emma's mask is so rigidly positioned that neither flexibility nor playfulness can disrupt her or deflect from her entrenched self-construction as an English spinster and bearer of enlightenment to the Afrikaners.

Yet the South African heat, the dust and the flat plains of the Karroo, the infestation of flies and mosquitoes, and the brutal and seemingly illogical acts of dog-whipping and cat-skinning by the earthy Afrikaners with whom she sojourns, burn off the mask as surely as Emma relinquishes her corset after fainting in the excruciating heat: 'What would Mama have said? For – as you know – she taught us that the correct corsetry could fortify one against hell itself' (de Wet 1995: 10). This regulation is graphically evoked in pictures of Victorian women. For Casey Finch 'the buxom, voluptuous . . . Renaissance ideal of the female body . . . was irrevocably overthrown during the Victorian period . . . and was replaced by the new hourglass shape as the desideratum [taken to an] extreme' (Finch 1991: 340–1). The evocation of this image emphasizes the bodily confinement that signifies both a fashion statement and protection against the anathema of sexual intimacy, which Emma terms 'depraved' (de Wet 1995: 10). Her dismay stems from what Bernard Rudofsky considers the prevailing middle-class perspective that 'an uncorsetted woman reeked of license; an unlaced waist was regarded as a vessel of sin' (Rudofsky 1972: 110–11). Emma's uncorseting, while a necessary strategy for adapting to the South African climate, also metaphorizes her now unguarded body and the potential for the release of her repressed sexuality. Katy, like Viola, performs the narration of her sister's story; unlike Viola's imagined sister, whom Lisa Jardine argues represents '"virtue" here . . . the silent enduring of whatever patriarchal fortune brings' (Jardine 1989: 182), Emma neither sits patiently nor smiles at her grief, since she is enveloped in a tortuous struggle with herself that is projected on to her employer, Mr Brand. In contrast to Viola, Emma chooses spiritual purity over bodily shame and commits suicide.

In de Wet's play with its all-female cast the two Victorian sisters explore only a partial range of emotions and issues as befits the prohibitions asserted by societal norms and internalized as self-inflicted repressions. This repressive atmosphere is also rendered concrete in the conduct of the Brands at table: the children speak only when spoken to and the servants are silent and submissive. The palpable presence of absent men pervades the text in diverse, revelatory modes. Mr Mackintosh, the wealthy suitor whom Emma rejects, epitomizes economic security and a civilized life in England. Katy's reminder to Emma, 'Be sensible and settle down . . . you are not getting any younger', provokes a definite reply: 'It is the act of physical intimacy . . . [that I find] humiliating and abhorrent' (10). Reggie is Katy's sexually demanding husband, whom she 'frequently reminds that moderation is the silken thread running through the pearl chain of our virtues' (10); this rejoinder foregrounds the masterful mimetic construction of one Victorian female voice and reminds us that gender oppression takes many forms and will certainly continue if women take refuge in silence or veiled objections. In Katy's view their father as parental authority wields ultimate power over his adult daughters and she thus gives him the letters and Emma's private journal: 'Papa, you have a right to know. The sacred right of a parent' (15). The play emphasizes the central position of men in society: bread-winners, providers of security, demanders of sexual favours, authority figures.

The object of Emma's suppressed desire in an ambivalent relationship of disgust and repulsion yet ever growing attraction, is the uncouth Afrikaner, Mr Brand, whose name in English signifies fire and burning, a policy employed in widespread destruction of Boer farms by the British during the Anglo-Boer war. In Emma's hallucinations Mr Brand inflicts fire and burning on her; even the red weals on her body signify the marks of ownership as certainly as cattle-branding and form a visual text of shame and violation. Foucault's observation that 'hysteria was perceived as the effect of an internal heat that spread throughout the body' (Foucault 1988: 139) provides another nominal signification, as do the intertextual resonances of a New Testament passage in which the apostle Paul advises single men and women:

> I say therefore to the unmarried and widows, It is good for them if they abide even as I. But if they cannot contain, let them marry: for it is better to marry than to burn.
>
> (I Corinthians 7: 8–9)

Emma's shame and guilt at her burning desire for Mr Brand is reflected in internalized and stigmatized images of 'burning' (both 'blushing' and the 'fires' of hell). The juxtaposition of the status of the two sisters interrogates the certitude of this injunction. Emma's unfulfilled desires that are rendered concrete in the enactment of hysteria, and Katy's conjugal duties that consign her to the status of a reproductive machine and produce ill-health, emphasize the tenuous position of women at the beginning of this century; resonances of patriarchal structures and gender differentials offer an uncomfortable reminder of what still exists today.

The play's curtain lines form Katy's well-rehearsed and dreamed-of response in an imagined confrontation with Mr Brand, who constitutes for the Victorian matron all that is villainous: 'he would feel my eyes burning into him . . . a flood of words would pour out of me . . . to express the abysmal . . . disgust I feel for him' (de Wet 1995: 30). This passionate outburst of counter-transference is performed in response to Miss Brand's letter, which Katy typically evaluates from a superior vantage point: 'A spidery scrawl on inferior paper. . . . The language – by the way – is extremely poor. But then what can you expect' (ibid.: 29). The readings of that letter speak volumes about the sender and the receiver. Mr Brand's imminent marriage to the neighbouring widow of a Boer soldier re-emphasizes how he perpetuates normative behaviour, which, in turn, makes of Emma the outsider. Miss Brand names no specific condition but suggests an awareness of Emma's problem: 'She was always looking at my brother. It made him ashamed. Sometimes she was very funny in the night' (ibid.: 29). Katy's outrage at this insinuation, however, involves a double perplexity: her straitlaced spinster sister's prurient desires being focused on an ill-smelling rough man and her realization that the enactment of these desires eschews conjugal duty and instead exhibits untrammelled sexual appetite. In addition, Miss Brand's intimations of Emma's neurosis and therefore, by implication, an inner weakness and a blighted mind, are the final straw that provokes what for Katy is a tirade, without any thorough reflection on the state of affairs. This singular perspective on the sisters and the conviction of the rectitude of their *modus vivendi* is at the core of the play; not only does it satirize the relationship between the English and the Boers, but perhaps more pertinently it encourages spectators to transpose that dynamic to the typical association between the Afrikaners and Blacks in the lived reality of an interregnum South Africa, where systemic injustices, power differentials, gross exploitations and the refusal to listen to voices and concerns have blighted the lives, burned the property and ignited an endemic conflagration of violence – in short, rendered no refuge for the individual or national home.

Emma attempts to stave off her growing disturbance after seeing Mr Brand's naked chest, her first view of a partially unclothed male body, and experiencing other instances of awakened desire that she neither understands nor accepts. She blames her indisposition on Mr Brand's unwanted attentions (ibid.: 16, 17, 20, 21, 27) and discloses her momentous struggle with herself: 'I shall elevate my thoughts and purify my mind by copying down more of Mr Shelley's immortal lines' (ibid.: 18). Her recitation of the second stanza of Shelley's 'To a Skylark' is a paean to joy and freedom. This construction of flight and freedom ironically comments on Emma's admiration of and complicity in societal structures that entrap her.

In *A Worm in the Bud* Emma's letters to Katy inform her about mundanities of her South African life in order to protect her pregnant sister in her 'delicate condition'. The journal entries, however, which allow her some outlet for her fears and desires, evoke in detail inner conflict and obsessive hallucinations. Recording her hallucinations on the page provides, on the one hand, an outlet for confrontation with that which appears so horrific and intensifies, on the other, the reality of her plight. Emma, seemingly certain of her shameful intimacy with Mr Brand and fearing the ramification of a monstrous pregnancy, sets the stage for her suicide: she dresses herself in full attire, drinks a bottle of laudanum and allows the powerful narcotic to complete its task. Even here the educated, cultured Emma re-enacts a scene worthy of a pre-Raphaelite painting and in fact emulates the death of Elizabeth Siddal, Dante Gabriel Rossetti's wife, whom she cites in the play. While Katy's letters inform Emma about other English visitors abroad whose illnesses have been cured on their return to England by local doctors, Emma has neither an English doctor nor anyone nearby whom she trusts; accordingly, she turns away from the vile Afrikaner folk medicines, resorts to her own remedy, and seeks ultimate refuge in the staging of a final performance that silences her 'speaking' body and covers the burns that mark her fall into disgrace.

The audience as analyst of Emma's malady, whether it is categorized as an illness, a discursive construct, or a site of power struggles, witnesses the material consequences and confronts the silencing of women's voices, the divisiveness of societal structures, and her inability to make of home a refuge. In *A Worm in the Bud* spectators are interpellated by competing ideologies and issues from the turn of the century. As it questions societal practices operating then, so the play also exposes similarities in the current dynamics of oppression, the hierarchical power networks, and the problematics of home; these issues are as relevant now as they were then, but perhaps in contemporary times they are more directly articulated and more vigorously resisted. Interpretations of the play and its relevance to conditions in South African society take on added significance when Chaudhuri's notion that identity is a function of place is situated in conjunction with Foucault's assertion that 'who one is . . . emerges acutely out of the problems with which one struggles' (Rabinow 1994: xix). Now that the interregnum era of the play's opening production has passed into a post-election phase, it is more urgent to extrapolate de Wet's contention that Emma exemplifies the principle that 'if you repress something it will shatter you. Any deep repression that is never faced will destroy you' (quoted in Huismans and Finestone 1995: 94). When home is no refuge either corporeally or nationally, then disaster looms. Awareness of varying networks of power and a readiness to rethink and experience the value of difference instead of otherness is an ongoing process that can ultimately make of the home a refuge, whether writ small or large.*

* Sincere thanks to Reza de Wet for supplying the unpublished manuscript of the play and for the opportunities for discussion. My appreciation to Terry Goldie, Ian Sowton and Hersh Zeifman for their comments on an earlier version of this article and to Stephen Barber for an enriching dialogue with my work. My gratitude to the Social Sciences and Humanities Council of Canada for a postdoctoral fellowship that supports my work at the Open University in the UK.

REFERENCES

Adler, Michelle (1996) 'Skirting the edges of civilization: two Victorian women travellers and "colonial spaces" in South Africa', in Kate Darian-Smith, Liz Gunner and Sarah Nuttall (eds) *Text, theory, space*, London: Routledge.

Auerbach, Nina (1982) *Woman and the Demon: The Life of a Victorian Myth*, London: Harvard University Press.

Balme, Jennifer Hobhouse (1994) *To Love One's Enemies*, Cobble Hill, British Columbia: Hobhouse Trust.

Blumberg, Marcia (1993) 'Dialogue with Reza de Wet', unpublished (10 July).

Blumberg, Marcia (forthcoming 1998) 'Interview with Reza de Wet', *South African Theatre As/And Intervention*, ed. Marcia Blumberg and Dennis Walder, Amsterdam: Rodopi.

Chaudhuri, Una (1995) *Staging Place: the Geography of Modern Drama*, Ann Arbor, MI: University of Michigan Press.

de Wet, Reza (1995) 'A worm in the bud', in *Open Spaces*, ed. Yvette Hutchinson and Kole Omotoso, Groote Schuur, Cape: Kagiso Press, pp.1–30.

Finch, Casey (1991) '"Hooked and buttoned together": Victorian underwear and representations of the female body', *Victorian Studies* 34(3): 337–63.

Fisher, John (1971) *That Miss Hobhouse*, London: Secker & Warburg.

Foucault, Michel (1988) *Madness and Civilization: A History of Insanity in the Age of Reason*, New York: Vintage Books.

Foucault, Michel (1990) *The History of Sexuality*, Vol. 1, trans. Robert Hurley, New York: Vintage.

Freedman, Barbara (1991) *Staging the Gaze*, Ithaca, NY: Cornell University Press.

Gramsci, Antonio (1971) *Selections from the Prison Notebooks of Antonio Gramsci*, ed. and trans. Quintin Hoare and Geoffrey Nowell Smith, New York: International Publishers.

Hewison, Hope Hay (1980) *Hedge of Wild Almonds: South Africa, the Pro-Boers & the Quaker Conscience 1890–1910*, London: James Curry.

Huismans, Anja and Finestone, Juanita (1995) 'Interview: Anja Huismans and Juanita Finestone talk to Reza de Wet', *South African Theatre Journal* 9(1)(May): 89–95.

Jardine, Lisa (1989) *Still Harping on Daughters*, New York: Columbia University Press.

Mohanty, Chandra Talpede (1991) 'Cartographies of struggle: Third World women and the politics of feminism', in *Third World Women and the Politics of Feminism*, ed. Chandra Mohanty, Ann Russo and Lourdes Torres, Bloomington, IN: Indiana University Press.

Pearsall, Ronald (1993[1969]) *The Worm in the Bud: The World of Victorian Sexuality*, London: Pimlico.

Rabinow, Paul (1994) 'Introduction: the history of systems of thought', in Michel Foucault, *Ethics: Subjectivity and Truth*, Vol. 1, ed. Paul Rabinow, New York: New Press, pp. xi–xli.

Rudofsky, Bernard (1972) *The Unfashionable Human Body*, London: Hart-Davis.

Shakespeare, William (1975) *Twelfth Night*, Arden edition, London: Methuen.

Sibley, David (1995) *Geographies of Exclusion: Society and Difference in the West*, London: Routledge.

Sichel, Adrienne (1990) 'Windybrow premiere for Reza de Wet's satire on colonial philanthropists', *Pretoria News*, 13 February: n.p.

Stevenson, Robert Louis (1905) *A Child's Garden of Verses*, New York: Charles Sonbrey.

Vicinus, Martha (1973) 'Introduction', in *Suffer and Be Still: Women in the Victorian Age*, ed. Martha Vicinus, Bloomington, IN: Indiana University Press.

Wren, Celia (1990) 'Colonial dream versus Africa's spirit in new play', *Weekly Mail*, 9–15 March: 21.

after the hunt

after Ovid

It begins with the end of the hunt
Around midday when shadows are too thin
To hide in from the hard heat of the sun
In a field between forest and forest
Actaeon is speaking to his party
WE HAVE KILLED MORE THAN ENOUGH FOR TODAY
OUR NETS ARE FULL BLADES POLISHED WITH THE BLOOD
OF OUR GAME AND NOW THE SWELTERING SKY
BURNS THE STONES BENEATH OUR FEET IT'S TIME
TO HEAD FOR HOME BUT TOMORROW AT DAWN
WE'LL BE BACK TO HUNT AGAIN Not that I
Up high on the platform of my tower
Heard one word of what he said though it's bound
To have been something along those lines
In this happy scene of fond farewells
Not so far south in a narrow valley
Lies carved out of the rock by nature's artists
Wind and rain a grotto and before it
Mostly hidden by a waterfall sleeps
A small lagoon where Diana goddess
Of the hunt but also protector of the shy
And defenceless creatures of the woods
Often tired from her sport comes to bathe and
Cool her naked beauty pampered by her nymphs
One holds her spear and bow and quiver others

The large print on these six pages is a verse text by Marc von Henning for a performance by **primitive science** at the Spital Studio in London at the end of July. It is a reworking of Ovid's version of the story of the death of Actaeon, who was devoured by his own hounds as a punishment for having gazed even innocently, even accidentally, on the naked breast of the goddess Diana. To say as much is enough to make it difficult to continue. Even to utter the name. How can I? Ovid wrote twisted tales of wonderful transformations, precariously linked by confusion. Gods turn into humans, humans into animals trees and stone, often as

Fold her gowns over their arms and loosen
a punishment, but sometimes also as a means of
The sandals from her weary feet but
escape: after all, nothing can happen to you once you've
It is Crocale with her gifted hands
been turned to a stone or crushed blue steel. The idea
Who carefully untangles the long hair
was to have been to extend the performance text for the
Of this divine creature and weaves it
page, to turn it back to paper and then to elaborate upon
Into plaits while five younger naiads Nephele
it by adding a bigger range of cultural references, by
Hyale Phiale Psecas Rhanis
turning perhaps to the wonderful painting by Titian
Pour water over Diana's body
called The Death of Actaeon or to earlier and later
A heavenly sight though I would not dare
translations of Ovid's text or to Elias Canetti's
Disclose to others that I've witnessed it
dissertation on flight and transformation in Crowds
She would surely have me fed to her bears
and Power. The central notion was to have been 'in
Then from nowhere I see him approaching
betweenness', in betweenness being in myth the site of
Actaeon in an idle stroll through woods
magical transformation–the crossroads–the ford– the
And fields of his estate unknown to him
waterfall; in betweenness being also a place or moment
He stumbles on the grotto and its secret pool
of refuge. Then there was the in betweenness of all
Then out of the blue I watch him driven
stories to be examined, between the private experience
By innocent curiosity I suppose
of an event and the public knowing of it. 'It would be
Step through the falling water and its spray
boring just to retell Ovid's tale,' von Henning wrote
And stand before the nymphs all naked
about the setting of his little play, 'but in the form of a
My queen it cannot be a crime to lose
secret witness having to report it to a third party it gains
Your way in unfamiliar territory
an extra dimension, then in the fact that the witness
Destiny not design is to blame for
must rehearse the story to himself to build up his
Actaeon's error today after all
confidence to report it.'
Nature does not obey our notion of ethics

It is expected that like six photographers and a motorcycle messenger detained at the scene, they will be placed under formal examination for manslaughter, recklessly causing injury and failing to offer assistance after an accident. The owner of the agency employing two of the men, Laurent Sola of LS Presse, confirmed yesterday that he had marketed pictures of the wrecked car, including five close-ups of Diana injured in the wreckage. He said that as soon as he heard Diana was dead, he withdrew the pictures from the market. Mr Sola said that he saw nothing wrong on the night in selling the pictures because you could 'recognise her perfectly. She is pretty in the picture. There is just a little thing in her left eye.'[1]

Its cruelty is unpredictable
So there were to have been two rooms. You might
And indiscriminate not calculated
imagine them shimmering on the page rather like
And addressed *-pause-*
the animated sequences one finds these days in
The nymphs panic beat their breasts and scream
multimedia encyclopaedias: in one room a queen
Their faces torn in terror huddling quick
expecting Actaeon, her lover, to return from the
Round their mistress as though to be her costume
hunt; in the other adjoining, a messenger,
But it's no good she is too tall for them
dumbstruck from the hunt, bearing the news of
To screen THAT BOEOTIAN NUMBSKULL
Actaeon's accidental encounter with Diana and her
WHO STANDS THERE IN THE BUSHES OGLING
nymphs and all its terrible consequences. Here are
Of course nothing is more painful to
the rooms as you might imagine them, different
The goddess of the hunt than a man's eyes
worlds with a common dividing wall: here, the queen
On her white skin it turns her into prey
dressing, arranging the furniture, choosing music,
Her cheeks blush like an early cloud at dawn
imagining herself seducer and seduced; here, her
Or one that's still in the sky at sunset
messenger, fidgeting, sighing, pacing, lighting then
She looks around but no weapon is at hand
stamping out cigarettes half-smoked, or scrawling
No arrows to drill through his body only
on the floorboards, or arranging the furniture to
Water at her knees and she scoops up
remake the death-scene, or pressing his fists
A handful and flings it into his eyes
together in front of his eyes. And at the end of the
I hear her speak to him the voice of
sequence, where the text ends and the reality of the
Immortals of course is not dulled by distance
encounter between the two players must begin,
NOW IF YOU CAN, GO AND BRAG TO YOUR FRIENDS
perhaps a picture of a door opening between the
THAT I ALLOWED YOU TO SEE ME NAKED.
ante-room and the queen's forbidden chamber. Since
From now I will have to charge my report
which, and obscuring everything, an extreme,
With more emotion to boost the tragedy–

My heart my queen I swear it stopped as it
astonishing transformation: the story of Diana
Does now. Suddenly his neck stretches out
and Actaeon is tipped on its head or bursts
His back narrows his hands turn hooves his arms
inside out or bulges in mirror image.
Into long legs his ears pointed his skin
I wouldn't dream of pretending to know what
Soon burns to hide and from his forehead grows
slant to put on this new conjunction, between
A rack of antlers Royal Actaeon
the death of Actaeon and now the death of this
Is transformed into a stag Have my eyes
other Diana, so many and so preposterous are
Misunderstood THOSE MOST THEORETICAL
the connections between the two stories: the
OF ORGANS where the senses meet the soul.
pups and paps, the taxi driver's reference
Actaeon is sweating fear it's time to wake up
(given somewhere below) to the panic among
Out of his nightmare no nightmare though
hunted deer, the journey into the underworld
He leaps out of the grove himself
beneath the Place de L'Alma. There can be no
Bewildered by the lightness of his step
connection–of course not; no connection, as
I follow his path through the clearing and
the whole world skids into a crevasse of
Up the hillside where among some trees
fictions. The point is only that the story of
He jolts to a halt in front of a stream
Diana and Actaeon we meant to tell no longer
In it he sees reflected his new image
bears unravelling. One simply cannot tell it,
The antlered head. Terrified he screams out
or illustrate it or extend it or explore its
But no words want to cross his lips only
resonances, so huge so crazy so bewildering
A deep rutting from his aching lungs
so sprawling is the new myth that has
But there is one thing that has not changed
consumed it.
The tears running down his face are human still
Which is which? When she was sitting on her
I could see Actaeon trapped in hesitation
father's knee and was asked what presents she
Caught between shame and fear. Should he run back

entered the expanse of the Place de la Concorde where the traffic flows four or five cars abreast over the cobblestones. Here the security guard substituted for the chauffeur is believed to have hit the accelerator. But his attempt to outpace the photographers failed: after all, they were old hands at the deadly game. The Mercedes sped on towards the River Seine. The dual carriageway exits to the west, along the Cours de la Reine, funnels the vehicles into a narrower raceway with a low central dividing wall. The temptation here is to accelerate, although the speed limit is normally between 50 and 70km an hour. There is, first, one shallow underpass, illuminated by yellow strip lighting from the frosted glass panels to the side. 'You should never drive along there too fast,' a woman taxi driver said yesterday. 'Take care when you approach the second tunnel. It swings to the left just as you go

Here to the palace or hide in the forest
Whether it was his rutting as he tried
To scream or whether the hounds had simply
Caught his scent now they're on his trail
Panting slobbering fleshing their teeth barking
You know them well don't you my queen Tracker
The Cretan hound Blackfoot from Sparta swift
As the wind and Nape whose mother was
A wolf then Hunter the keenest nose Snatch
With her two pups and Barker noisy bitch
All together like a hurricane howling
Through the woods in pursuit of their master
Where he had often worked his hounds so hard
To make them catch the prey he now works
So hard to shake them off his own heels
Desperate his attempt to shout out at them
I AM ACTAEON YOUR KING AND MASTER
His tongue though carries only dead noises.
Now you must sit to hear the final part
And hear it you must though I don't want to
Speak it. The first to feel him in the trap
Of her jaws is Snatch a deep wound she bites
Into his haunch then Killer the wise dog
Who has cut across the hills to snarl him

would like, which Diana said to her father,
'Daddy, give me eternal virginity, the office of
bringing light; a saffron tunic with a red hem
reaching to my knees; all the mountains in the
world; and any city you care to choose for me,
but one will be enough, because I intend to live
on mountains most of the time.[2] Enquire what
the press-hounds were like. Were they not white
with red ears, in every detail resembling the
hounds of Hell? One asks the night before the
London funeral, knowing full well that between
now and the moment when these pages are
published, in that in betweenness, the storm of
storytelling and retelling will have increased in
force, that these overlaps and confusions will
have been washed up in a hundred languages on
a hundred shores, that there will be no escape
from them except in blankness.

down. There have been accidents there before.'
Another chauffeur said later: 'You need to
practise in driving like that, you need to be a
professional driver for the job. Perhaps he was
driving too fast, like Grace of Monaco. If you
know the job, you get used to the paparazzi.
So they take their pictures; she had nothing to
escape from. But maybe they were like deer
being hunted, in a panic. If you drive at
160km an hour, it's not a small curve
approaching that underpass. You can't make
it at that speed.'[3]

Fastens tight on his shoulder. He falls
Struggles hard but they hold him down until
The whole pack arrives and united as one
In the kill sink their teeth into his flesh
The wail that spurts from his mouth with his blood
Is not human neither though a sound
A stag could make and as his hunters reach
The scene he has no more strength but to wave
His head in silence side to side but they
Thrilled by the work their dogs have done leave them
To rip him limb from limb One I can't see
Which tears his heart from the open breast
And runs with it into the nearby cave
So as not to have to share the precious part
The hunters ignorant of course call out
For their king and friend to celebrate
With them the unexpected kill and what
A beautiful beast. On no-one not even
Actaeon the patron saint of Peeping Toms
Would I wish such a death slaughtered
At the hands of murderers he had himself
Instructed in the art of killing.
And is it not the fate of every hunter
That one day he will become the hunt

Marc von Henning / Kevin Mount 1997

A person in a state of melancholia feels that pursuit is over and he has already been captured. He cannot escape; he cannot find fresh metamorphoses. Everything he attempted has been in vain; he is resigned to his fate and sees himself as prey: first as prey, then as food, and finally as carrion or excrement. The process of depreciation, which makes his own person seem more and more worthless, is figuratively expressed as feelings of guilt. Guilt was originally the same as debt (in German there is still only one word for them both). If one is in debt to someone one is to that extent in his power. Feeling guilty and thinking of oneself as prey are thus basically the same. The melancholic does not want to eat, and as a reason for his refusal may say that he does not deserve to. But the real reason is that he sees himself as being eaten, and, if forced to eat, is reminded of this. His own mouth turns against him; it is as though a mirror were held before him and he saw a mouth in it, and saw that something was being eaten. But this something is himself.[4]

SOURCES

[1] *adapted from* The Guardian, September 1st 1997
[2] *see* Robert Graves, The Greek Myths, Vol 1, Penguin Books, 1955
[3] The Guardian, *ibid.*
[4] Elias Canetti, Crowds and Power, Victor Gollancz, London 1962

Who is Lili Fischer?

Kirsten Winderlich

I'm turning to you with an art project: I've just developed a collection of artistic equipment for domestic use – e.g. an *Begleitrolle* ('Accompanying Roll') for your water tap (a 10m roll showing a painted water cycle), *Klassische Hausgeister* ('Classic House Spirits'; shadows of famous people), a *Spinnweben-Quintett* ('Spiderweb Quintet') or the *Seufzenden Waschepuff* ('Groaning Laundry Basket'). These are all objects to be installed directly in the house, the hall, the living-room, the kitchen – and not in a gallery. The idea is to artistically illuminate the domestic environment – in the broadest sense of the word. This project, by the way, is an experiment supported by the Ministry of Education and Science. I would like to ask you now, if you are interested in me visting you at home. . . . With kind regards, Lili Fischer.

(Fischer 1989: 1)

She goes away to the outer Hebrides. She is there on her own, she makes a home for herself in a peat hut. She walks around outside, takes photographs and does some drawing. In the evening she studies books about the islands and makes a peat fire.

. . . **simply that [*einfach so*].**

Lili Fischer's way of working – as she herself points out – is a kind of field research. She says: 'Field research means that you focus on a certain field, an object from which, then, asthetic dimensions are derived and investigated; one after the other, without any frantic force to gain an artistic result . . . simply that.' In regard to Lili Fischer's working methods and her use of language, 'simply that' is a very informative phrase. She uses it a lot. Many of this artist's books and scripts end with 'simply that' drawings. In everyday language, 'simply that' seems to mean that something is done optionally, without any sense, without an aim. At university, to give 'simply that' as a reason for a research project would be absolutely unthinkable. These three words work as a metaphor of Lili Fischer's field research, of what characterizes all her performances. The words are a metaphor, on one hand, of seeming chance and, on the other, of a pointed grip on things by employment of drawings, photographs, objects, texts and her own person. Nothing that Lili Fischer presents in her performances is optional; all is prepared and planned. Her scripts, in which she fixes every single step, every single word, clarify exactly this. Within the context of Lili Fischer's work, 'simply that' is not an empty phrase, but a stimulus to move further towards the unexpected and unconventional. Lili Fischer's 'simply that' envisages modes of investigation that one can find only by letting go of the idea of achieving a result.

Lili Fischer's way of working includes artistic methods as well as those used, for example, in ethnology. There such research methods always lead to a reduction of reality: enacted by decisions on a specific topic and the chosen mode of investigation, the reflective subjectivity of the investigator, and various conditions of the research process and scientific terminology. In her field research projects, Lili Fischer does not reduce reality in order either to gain unambiguous results or to describe and present an unambiguous reality (as all

Performance Research 2(3), pp.45-49 © Routledge 1997

empirical sciences would do). She rather reduces her field of investigation in order to reopen it – by playfully developed, not always foreseeable approaches, transferring it into other forms of possibility. Such unexpected forms of possibility become visible when she describes geological layers of clay, shell and peat as 'layers of ideas' (Fischer 1982: 2); or when she depicts the movements done in cleaning as measurable lines and calculable distances.

Lili Fischer's work is focused on marginal realms: landscape or household. In her performances, through her transferring these realms into new or lost forms of possibility, the field itself comes to be understood as a model. The field, then, is a consciously delineated slice of life that is investigated in terms of its conditions and structures. When Lili Fischer explores these actual localities, she employs certain methods to develop a database – e.g. participating observation and interview – that is used in all empirical sciences. Her next step is to document all data in different ways and materials: notes, drawings, objects, photos, tapes. Through this, she makes visible forgotten or unexpectedly new connections between people, everyday life, history and nature; she enacts contact with lives and realities; she provides new perspectives. In her performances the audience is asked to contribute information which becomes part of the artwork itself. In her research, Lili Fischer never relies on herself alone.

She pays domestic visits. She turns up at the doors of houses in Hamburg-Fuhlsbüttel and asks for old brushes, sponges and cloths. She says she is doing an 'offertory' of old scrubbing equipment and offers cleaning tools in exchange.

HAWKING

An 'offertory' is a collection, usually of money, and usually for a good cause. People generally contribute something without getting anything in exchange. Although it is uncommon, Lili Fischer offers some service in return. Her extra offer makes it possible for her to collect more scrubbing equipment in less time. Moreover, she confronts people with ancient forms of life-keeping, and allows them to be trading partners on equal terms. In this way she also spares herself the role of 'the obtrusive hawker'.

Lili Fischer says that old brushes are valuable, because they are the only evidence of our everyday cleaning activities. Here, she proposes a shift of values: in exchanging old cleaning tools that are no longer usable, for brand-new brushes, sponges and cloths, she turns those used-up objects into items worthy of collection.

Lili Fischer does not put on her usual clothes when she pays those visits, but masquerades as a hawker: she wears a brown suit, a brown hat and a shoulder-bag. She raises people's curiosity by obviously playing a role. It is, after all, her masquerade that shows she does not want to do business, but wants to demonstrate something that involves those being visited as audience as well as co-actors. Lili Fischer invites people in Hamburg-Fuhlsbüttel to look at a series of images showing

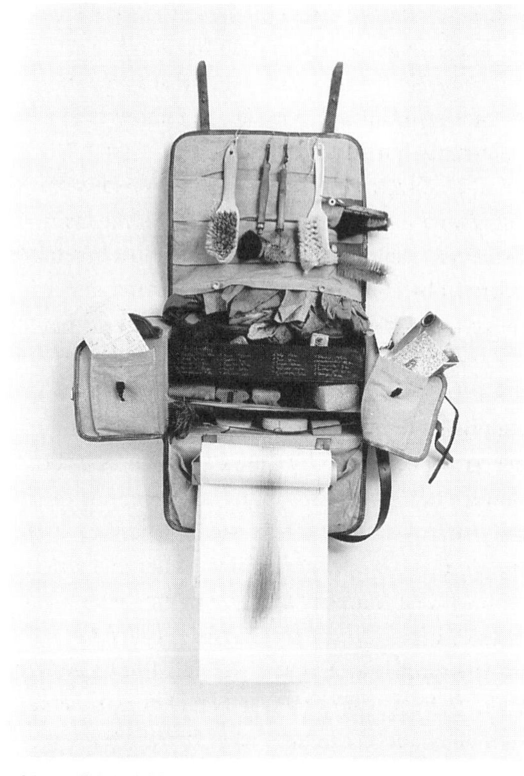

• *Scheuermittelkollekte* ('Scrubbing Equipment'), Lili Fischer, 1986. Photo: Lili Fischer

centres of dirt, and she shows diagrams which picture the distances we cover in our daily cleaning activities; cleaning the lavatory, for example, takes 12 metres. People, thus, are confronted with a common everyday task presented in different ways and from different perspectives: the place of action is represented as a series of photographs, the time taken is pictured in linear units of measurement – and there is a real person, Lili Fischer in masquerade, who has already had some experience with that action and therefore could be asked.

People come to recognize her as someone who deals with an everyday duty quite differently from the way they do. The concept of cleaning as an everyday action, here, is turned into a special, extraordinary doing that has not been experienced as such before. People might think and ask: 'Is scubbing anything else but a necessary evil?' There is somebody showing an interest in dirt, in the circumstances of its removal! This, here, foregrounds a process that is usually silent and hidden from the public. Where can I find such centres of dirt? For how long have they not been cleaned ? How can I work out scrubbing distances? When I do my cleaning, do I destroy something that is worth keeping? Am I doing something extraordinary when scrubbing? All this raises the question of what 'cleaning' actually is; what is happening when one cleans, what its effects are and what value it has. This uncertainty is, at the same time, counterbalanced by Lili Fischer's demonstration of 'cleaning' as a phenomenon that can be represented and measured, and whose effects can be visualized. Lili Fischer raised data, collected comparative material and presented it. She asked cleaning people about their activities and documented their statements.

It would, of course, be possible for Lili Fischer to introduce herself as a professional investigator, with a proper questionnaire and the confirmation of an official institution. She could ask people's permission to show photos, collect used scrubbing equipment, ask questions and tape them for later use. But something else is at stake here: the meaning of the action itself. This is clarified at the end of the hawker's commentary as she shows her '*Putzfahrten*' (literally, 'scrubbing tours').

'*Putzfahrten*' are scrubbing movements which are given form in lines, ellipses and spirals. They embody the fusion of location, action and movement. Cleaning becomes a picture. In her performance Lili Fischer calls these drawings 'the original forms of the coming into being of our solar system'. This image provides a hint at the originality and vital necessity of that action. In the end, as it turns out that Lili Fischer can imagine *anything* as an explanation or description of scrubbing, she asks: 'Of what do you think when you do the cleaning?'

Of course this question could be part of a questionnaire, but in such a form she would not get answers like this one from an elderly man: 'Scrubbing? I have nothing to do with that . . . I am alone. My wife died four years ago, I have nothing to do with that any more, I don't know anything about it; four years ago my wife died.'

• *Klärschlamm* ('Charleston'), Lili Fischer, 1987. Photo: Hinrich Sachs

A questionnaire as the carrier of that question would provide too little concreteness, too little space for an individual answer and too much space for excuses. Lili Fischer's performance, though, enables people to consider the multiplicity of meanings of 'cleaning' which are opened up in various personal encounters and dialogues.

Through questioning cleaning she works as a mythologist. As a mythologist she discloses the myth of 'cleaning', breaks it into parts and hence opens it up to various meanings.

TOWARDS AN AFTER-IMAGE

Roland Barthes suggested that everyday experiences and phenomena become myths through the erasure of history (Barthes 1994). Lili Fischer refers to the history of cleaning by employing her artistic methods on different levels: drawing, photograph, object, text and the investment of her own body work as a mode of instrumentalization. It is an aid to empathy, a means of imagination, an instrument of reflection and control; and it is the basis for the development of her performances. The employment of those methods always serves communication and dialogue – be it with herself, with her field of research, with the audience. Although employed as instruments, drawings, photographs, objects, text and her own self are simultaneously independent artistic statements.

Lili Fischer divides the myth of 'cleaning' into three levels. She develops, during her field research, a plan through confrontation with her surroundings (notes, diaries). She makes her results approachable for an audience and develops them further by including the audience's active participation (installation, performances). She collects and documents all that happens during her fieldwork as well as during her performances (scripts, artist's books).

Those levels of her artistic activities are not to be misunderstood as self-contained hierachically ordered and linear steps that build up towards an artistic result, but rather as interacting elements of a cyclical process of production, which is in permanent change. These modes of interaction turn Lili Fischer's research work into an 'event' – an event that enables the audience to consider its own use of language.

By speaking almost uninterruptedly during her home visits, she gives 'cleaning' varied meanings and discloses vanished contexts. While doing so she transforms the myth of 'cleaning' into particular unique stories.

AT HOME

The interview provides the setting for this event. However, Lili Fischer's interview is not intended to be an exchange of questions and answers between her and the audience. It appears as if Lili Fischer speaks almost uninterruptedly. But it is exactly this apparent monologue that relieves the audience from having to react verbally. She encourages the discovery and expression of one's own unique stories. Lili Fischer manages this first by alienating an object of her field that irritates the audience and tempts it to a new perception; then by demythologizing the object while yet giving it unusual meanings; and lastly by offering the audience its own language through this variety of meanings.

Lili Fischer alienates 'cleaning' by introducing it with an unexpected action and an unexpected comment. She achieves that, for instance, by collecting old scrubbing brushes and by declaring them to be valuable collector's items. The irritation of the audience – accompanied by the alienation – gives the audience space for reflection on its own personal cleaning story and gives the own cleaning experience special emphasis.

Lili Fischer demythologizes 'cleaning' and simultaneously opens it for a variety of meanings by decorating it with playful language and archetypal meanings: a laundry basket becomes a 'Groaning Laundry Basket' or a dirty table-cloth becomes a 'Hungercloth'. The objects are not seen as a given or taken for granted, but are described in their own historicity and in a new variety of meanings, as well. When giving a variety of meanings to objects, Lili Fischer does that from two angles: she shows the object both filled with sense and as an empty form. The empty form is to be seen, here, as space

• *Besentanz* ('Broomdance'), Lili Fischer, 1986. Photo: Kathrin Schneider.

for the language of the audience itself. The laundry basket, for example, is both filled with its own biography and empty in the sense of being open for the audience to make its individual perception of the object's meaning. Here, the meaning is the result of the activity of the audience.

And what do you think when you are cleaning . . . simply that?

Translated by Kerstin Brandes and Jürgen Amendinger

REFERENCES:

Barthes, Roland (1994) *Mythen des Alltags*, Frankfurt am Main: Suhrkamp.

Fischer, Lili (1982) *Dreckschweinfest/Watt & Weise*, Hamburg: Watt & Weise

Fischer, Lili (1989) *Hausieraktion in Künstlerisches Zubehör für Daheim*, Wiesbaden: Harlekin Art.

Against Ontology: Making Distinctions between the Live and the Mediatized

Philip Auslander

The prospectus for a Canadian conference on the topic 'Why Theatre: Choices for the New Century' posed a question that goes straight to the heart of the matter that concerns me here: 'Theatre and the media: rivals or partners?' At the level of cultural economy,* my own answer to this question is clear and unequivocal: theatre (and live performance generally) and the mass media are rivals, not partners. Neither are they equal rivals: it is absolutely clear that our current cultural formation is saturated with and dominated by the representations of the mass media. We have entered the era of what some theorists are calling the *televisual*. As Tony Fry puts it:

* I am using the phrase 'cultural economy' to describe a realm of inquiry that includes both the real economic relations among cultural forms and the relative degrees of cultural prestige and power enjoyed by different forms.

> What the televisual names . . . is the end of the medium, in a context, and the arrival of television as the context. What is clear is that television has to be recognised as an organic part of the social fabric; which means that its transmissions are no longer managed by the flick of a switch.
>
> (1993: 13)

In other words, if television once could be seen as ranking among a number of vehicles for conveying expression or information from which we could choose, we no longer have a choice; the televisual is an intrinsic and determining element of our cultural formation. As Fry indicates, it is indeed no longer a question of thinking about television in various cultural contexts but of seeing it as *the* cultural context.

My concern is with the situation of live performance within this televisual environment. In an earlier article, I described what I see as a pattern of increased incursion of mediatization into live events, and suggested that live events are largely losing their distinctive character as a result (see Auslander 1996). Despite this erosion of the differences between the live and the mediatized within our televisual culture, there remains a strong tendency in performance theory to place live performance and mediatized or technologized forms in opposition to one another. The terms of this opposition focus around two primary issues: *reproduction* and *distribution*.†

† I have borrowed these categories from Pavis (1992). They are two of fifteen vectors identified by Pavis along which live performance and media may be compared.

Herbert Molderings defines the question of reproduction by saying that 'in contrast to traditional art[,] performances do not contain a reproduction element. . . . Whatever survives of a performance in the form of a photograph or video tape is no more than a fragmentary, petrified vestige

Performance Research 2(3), pp.50-55 © Routledge 1997

of a lively process that took place at a different time in a different place' (1984: 172–3). Or, in Peggy Phelan's succinct formulations, performance 'can be defined as representation without reproduction' (1993a: 3); 'Performance's being becomes itself through disappearance' (1993a: 146). In terms of distribution, Patrice Pavis contrasts the one-to-many model of broadcasting with the 'limited range' of theatre: 'media easily multiply the number of their spectators, becoming accessible to a potentially infinite audience. If theatre relationships are to take place, however, the performance cannot tolerate more than a limited number of spectators' (1992: 101). In these formulations, live performance is identified with intimacy and disappearance, media with a mass audience, reproduction and repetition. Phelan offers an apt summary of this view: 'Performance honors the idea that a limited number of people in a specific time/space frame can have an experience of value which leaves no visible trace afterward' (1993a: 149).

Overtly or covertly, the writers I just quoted valorize the live over the mediatized, as is evident in Molderings's contrast between 'lively' performance and 'petrified' video. Even Pavis, who argues that theatre needs to be seen in relation to other media, nevertheless refers to the influence of other media on theatre as 'technological and aesthetic *contamination*' (1992: 134; my emphasis). All too often, such analyses take on the air of a melodrama in which virtuous live performance is threatened, encroached upon, dominated and contaminated by its insidious Other, with which it is locked in a life-and-death struggle. From this point of view, once live performance succumbs to mediatization, it loses its ontological integrity.

At one level, the anxiety of critics who champion live performance is understandable, given the way our cultural economy privileges the mediatized and marginalizes the live. In his analysis of the political economy of music, Jacques Attali describes the current historical configuration as dominated by a 'network of repetition' in which only mass-producible cultural commodities have value (1985: 87–132). In this account, live performance is little more than a vestigial remnant of the previous historical order, which can claim little in the way of cultural presence or power. Phelan claims that live performance's inability to participate in the economy of repetition 'gives performance art its distinctive oppositional edge' (1993a: 148). I would like to suggest in passing that in the context of a mediatized, repetitive economy, using the technology of reproduction in ways that defy that economy may be a more significantly oppositional gesture than asserting the value of the live. I am thinking, for instance, of Christine Kozlov's installation *Information: No Theory* (1970), which consisted of a tape recorder equipped with a tape loop, whose control was fixed in the 'record' mode. Therefore, as the artist herself noted, new information continuously replaced existing information on the tape, and 'proof of the existence of the information [did] not in fact exist' (in Meyer 1972: 172). The functions of reproduction, storage and distribution that animate the network of repetition were thus undermined by this way of using the very technology that brought that network into being.* In this context, reproduction without representation may be more radical than representation without reproduction.

* Attali (1985: 32) ascribes the development of the network of repetition to the invention of sound-recording technologies.

It is clear that the impulse to set live and mediatized forms in a relation of opposition is ideological in nature. Perhaps making a virtue of necessity, some theorists argue that live performance's existence on the margins of the economy of repetition makes it an oppositional discourse. Molderings describes performance art as a direct counter-response to television's banalization and objectification of the visual image (1984: 178–9). Phelan picks up this theme in a discussion of Anna Deveare Smith's *Twilight: Los Angeles, 1992*, suggesting that Smith's performance, which incorporates, alludes to and goes beyond the widely disseminated media images of the 1992 Los Angeles riots, 'seeks to preserve and contain the chaotic flood of images the cameras "mechanically" reproduced'. Phelan observes that this way of seeing the relationship between the live and the mediatized is based on 'an old boast – television cameras give you only "images," and theatre gives you living truth' and she emphasizes the degree to which Smith's performance is indebted to 'the camera that precedes and frames and invites' it (1993b: 6). She goes on to suggest that Smith's performance 'also offers another way to interpret the relation between film and theatrical performance: the camera's own performativity needs to be read as theatre' (1993b: 7).† Even though Phelan describes a subtle interaction between live and mediatized forms that goes beyond simple opposition, her suggestion that the action of the camera be seen as theatre tends to reinscribe the traditional privileging of the live over the mediatized: it is by entering the space of theatre, or being seen as theatre, that media images become subject to critique. I believe that the privileging of live performance as a site of critique is engrained to such a depth that were I to insist that the relationship between Smith's mediatized sources and her live performance suggests that we should see her performativity *as television*, that characterization would be thought to imply that her discourse cannot function critically.

†Phelan (1993b: 6) describes Smith's *Twilight* as signalling a shift in the relationship between television and theatre: 'formerly, live theatre hoped to find itself preserved on television, while Smith's performance transforms the "raw" televised story into stylized, well-rehearsed drama.' I tend to see Smith's work as belonging to a general cultural trend in which mediatized events are reconfigured as live ones. In the United States, this trend dates back at least to the mid-1950s, when television plays like *Twelve Angry Men* and *Visit to a Small Planet* were presented on Broadway, and has accelerated in recent times with the restaging of music videos as concerts and of cartoons as live musicals. In considering the relationship between theatre and television, does Smith's derivation of her performance from televisual documentary sources constitute a new development, or the extension of an established cultural trend into a new area?

My purpose here is to destabilize these theoretical oppositions of the live and the mediatized somewhat, first by reference to what might be called the 'electronic ontology' of media (these initial observations will not pertain to film, of course, whose ontology is photographic rather than electronic):

> the broadcast flow is . . . a vanishing, a constant disappearing of what has just been shown. The electron scan builds up two images of each frame shown, the lines interlacing to form a 'complete' picture. Yet not only is the sensation of movement on screen an optical illusion brought about by the rapid succession of frames: each frame is itself radically incomplete, the line before always fading away, the first scan of the frame all but gone, even from the retina, before the second interlacing scan is complete. . . . TV's presence to the viewer is subject to constant flux: it is only intermittently 'present,' as a kind of writing on the glass . . . caught in a dialectic of constant becoming and constant fading.
>
> (Cubitt 1991: 30–1)

As this quotation from Sean Cubitt suggests, disappearance may be even more fundamental to television than it is to live performance – the televisual image is always simultaneously coming into being and vanishing; there is no point at which it is fully present.* What presence it does possess is only a subjective effect created by the viewer's perceptual schema. At the electronic level, the televisual image is hardly a petrified remnant of some other event, as Molderings would have it, but exists rather as a lively, and forever unresolved, process. For some theorists, the televisual image's existence only in the present also obviates the notion that television (and video) is a form of reproduction. Contrasting television with film in this regard, Stephen Heath and Gillian Skirrow point out that

*** Kozlof's tape-recorder installation replicates this process of the continuous replacement of electronic information. The difference is that whereas in the normal usage of video this process is the necessary condition for the creation of a perceivable image, it becomes, when applied by Kozlof to sound recording, a way of making an imperceptible sound image that exists only theoretically.**

> where film sides towards instantaneous memory ('everything is absent, everything is *recorded* – as a memory trace which is so at once, without having been something else before') television operates much more as an absence of memory, the recorded material it uses – including material recorded on film – instituted as actual in the production of the television image.†
>
> (1977: 54–6)

Regardless of whether

†The quotation embedded in this quotation is from Christian Metz.

the image conveyed by television is live or recorded (and, as Stanley Cavell reminds us, on television there is 'no sensuous distinction between the live and the repeat or replay' [1982: 86]), its production as a televisual image occurs only in the present moment. 'Hence the possibility of *performing* the television image – electronic, it can be modified, altered, transformed in the moment of its transmission, is a production in the present' (Heath and Skirrow 1977: 53). Although Heath and Skirrow are referring here to broadcast television, what they say is as true for video as it is for broadcast: the televisual image is not only a reproduction or repetition of a performance, but a performance in itself.

If we shift our gaze from the electronic writing on the glass to consider, for a moment, the nature of the magnetic writing on a videotape, another issue comes to the fore. Cubitt posits as a crucial feature of the medium 'the phenomena of lost generations' resulting from the various stages of life a video image is likely to pass through, 'from master to submaster, to broadcast, to timeshift, where it begins to degenerate with every play' (1991: 169). Video shares this characteristic with other means of technical reproduction, including photographic and sound-recording media. Since tapes, films and other recording media deteriorate over time and with each use, they are, in fact, physically different objects at each playing, even though this process may only become visible when it reaches critical mass (e.g. when the film or video develops visible flaws). Each time I watch a videotape is the only time I can watch that tape in that state of being because the very process of playing it alters it. The tape that I initially placed in my VCR or audio-player started disappearing the moment I began watching it or listening to it. Disappearance, existence only in the present moment, is not, then, an ontological quality of live performance that distinguishes it from modes of technical reproduction. Both live performance and the performance of mediatization are predicated on disappearance: the televisual image is produced by an ongoing process in which scan lines replace one another and is always as absent as it is present; the use of recordings causes them to degenerate. In a very literal, material sense, televisual and other technical reproductions, like live performances, become themselves through disappearance.*

* It is worth wondering about the implications of digital reproductions for this position, since at least some digital media ostensibly do not degrade. My present feeling is that it is too soon to tell whether or not that's true.

I want to worry this question of reproduction in one last context, by considering the related issue of repetition. Writing on the experience of film, Cavell observes that

> movies . . . at least some movies, maybe most, used to exist in something that resembles [a] condition of evanescence, viewable only in certain places at certain times, discussable solely as occasions for sociable exchange, and never seen more than once, and then more or less forgotten.
>
> (1982: 78)

It is remarkable how closely Cavell's description of the film experience parallels descriptions of the experience of live performance. The fact that Cavell is talking about the past, probably about the heyday of the American film industry in the 1930s and 1940s, and about a way of experiencing film that we no longer believe to be typical, is critical. Film is no longer an unrepeated experience confined to particular places and times; people frequently see their favourite films multiple times, and have opportunities to do so afforded them by the movies' appearances on cable and broadcast television, and video-cassettes. If we want to, we can own copies of movies and watch them whenever, and as often as, we wish. Whereas film was once experienced as evanescence, it is now experienced as repetition. The crucial point is that this transition was not caused by any substantive change in the film medium itself. As a medium, film can be used to provide an evanescent experience that leaves little behind, in the manner of a live performance, or it can provide an experience based in repetition and the stockpiling of film commodities. Cubitt makes much the same point with respect to video, arguing that repetition is not 'an essence in the medium'. Rather, 'the possibility of repetition is only a possibility'; the actual use of the medium is determined by 'the imaginary relation of viewer and tape' (1991: 92–3). Repetition is not an ontological characteristic of either film or video that determines the experiences these media can provide, but an historically contingent effect of their culturally determined uses.*

*My insistence that how technologies are used should be understood as *effect* rather than *cause* derives from Raymond Williams's (1992) critique of technological determinism in *Television: Technology and Cultural Form* (Hanover, NH: Wesleyan University Press, pp. 113–28).

Just as recording media such as film and video can provide an experience of evanescence, so, too, live forms such as theatre have been used in ways that do not respect, or even recognize, the ostensible spatial and temporal characteristics of live performance. One such example would be the WPA Federal Theatre's 1936 production of *It Can't Happen Here*, which opened simultaneously in eighteen different American cities. The intention of this experiment is clearly suggested by a contemporary account which observes that the Federal Theatre produced the play 'after a motion picture corporation decided not to do it' (Whitman 1937: 6). To take a more current example, producers of the genre Elinor Fuchs has called 'shopping plays' envision live performances as repeatable commodities. Barrie Wexler, the California producer of *Tamara*, 'franchises . . . *Tamara* worldwide, replicating the product in exact and dependable detail. "It's like staying in the Hilton," he explains, "everything is exactly the same no matter where you are"' (Fuchs 1996: 142). In both these cases, live performance takes on the defining characteristics of a mass medium: it makes the same text available simultaneously to a large number of participants distributed widely in space. In fact, Hollywood saw the Federal Theatre as a competitor, and opposed it (Whitman 1937: 130–2). (I am not suggesting that there would be no differences between the various productions of a mass-media theatre production, such as *Tamara*. But if we take its producer at his word, whatever differences there might be would be trivial variations, not distinctions that would differentiate one production from another in any significant way.) It is crucial to observe that the intentions underlying these two examples of this use of the live medium are very different, and each is arguably reflective of its historical moment. Whereas the Federal Theatre Project's practices grew out of a generally left-populist attitude, shopping theatre 'mimics in its underlying structures of presentation and reception the fundamental culture of contemporary capitalism' (Fuchs 1996: 129). The ideological positioning of these productions is determined not by their shared use of live performance as a mass medium, but by the different intentions and contexts of those uses. Ironically, shopping plays like *Tamara* commodify the very aspects of live performance that are said to resist commodification. Because they are designed to offer a different experience at each visit, they can be merchandised as events that must be purchased over and over again: the ostensible evanescence and non-repeatability of the live experience become selling-points. This may be what Fuchs has in mind when she says that 'In this theater . . . we are seeing the commodification of the theatrical unconscious' (1996: 129).

I am suggesting that thinking about the relationship between live and mediatized forms in terms of ontological oppositions is not especially productive, because there are few grounds on which to make significant ontological distinctions. Like live performance, electronic and photographic media can be described meaningfully as partaking of the ontology of disappearance ascribed to live performance, and can be used to provide an experience of evanescence. Like film and television, theatre can be used as a mass medium. Half jokingly, I might cite Pavis's observation that 'theatre repeated too often deteriorates' (1992: 101) as evidence that the theatrical object degenerates in a manner akin to a recorded object! The more serious point is that to understand the relationship between live and mediatized forms, it is necessary to investigate that relationship as historical and contingent, not as ontologically given or technologically determined.

As a starting-point for this exploration, I have proposed (in Auslander 1996) that, historically, the live is an effect of mediating technologies. Prior to the advent of those technologies (e.g. sound recording and motion pictures), there was no such thing as 'live' performance, for that category has meaning only in relation to an opposing possibility. The ancient Greek theatre, for example, was not live because there was no possibility of recording it. In a special case of Baudrillard's well-known dictum that 'the very definition of the real is *that of which it is possible to give an equivalent reproduction*' (1983: 146), the 'live' can be defined only as '*that which can be recorded*'. (Although I realize that this is a contentious point, I will stipulate that I do not consider writing to be a form of recording in this context, for several reasons. Scripts are blueprints for performances, not recordings of them, even though they may contain some information based on performance practice. Written descriptions and drawings or paintings of performances are not direct transcriptions through which we can access the performance itself, as are aural and visual recording media. In everyday usage, we refer to 'live' or 'recorded' performances but not to written performances or painted performances, perhaps for this reason.) This means that the history of live performance extends over approximately the past 100 to 150 years, and is bound up with the history of recording media. To declare retroactively that all performance before, say, the mid-nineteenth century was 'live' would be an anachronistic imposition of a modern concept on a pre-modern phenomenon.

On this basis, the historical relationship of liveness and mediatization must be seen as a relation of dependence and imbrication rather than opposition. Similarly, live performance cannot be said to have ontological or historical priority over mediatization, since the live was brought into being by the possibility of technical reproduction. This problematizes Phelan's claim that 'To the degree that live performance attempts to enter into the economy of reproduction it betrays and lessens the promise of its own ontology' (1993a: 146), not just because it is not at all clear that live performance has a distinctive ontology, but also because it is not a question of performance's *entering into* the economy of reproduction, since it has always been there. My argument is that the very concept of live performance presupposes that of reproduction, that the live can exist only *within* an economy of reproduction.

REFERENCES

Attali, Jacques (1985) *Noise: The Political Economy of Music*, trans. Brian Massumi, Minneapolis: University of Minnesota Press.

Auslander, Philip (1996) 'Liveness: performance and the anxiety of simulation', in *Performance and Cultural Politics*, ed. Elin Diamond, London and New York: Routledge, pp. 198–213.

Baudrillard, Jean (1983) *Simulations*, trans. P. Foss, P. Patton and P. Beitchman, New York: Semiotext(e).

Cavell, Stanley (1982) 'The fact of television', *Daedalus* 111(4): 75–96.

Cubitt, Sean (1991) *Timeshift: On Video Culture*, London and New York: Routledge.

Fry, Tony (1993) 'Introduction', in *R U A TV?: Heidegger and the Televisual*, ed. Tony Fry, Sydney: Power Publications.

Fuchs, Elinor (1996) *The Death of Character: Perspectives on Theater after Modernism*, Bloomington, IN: Indiana University Press.

Heath, Stephen and Skirrow, Gillian (1977) 'Television, a world in action', *Screen* 18(2): 7–59.

Meyer, Ursula (1972) *Conceptual Art*, New York: E. P. Dutton.

Molderings, Herbert (1984) '*Life is No Performance*: Performance by Jochen Gerz', in *The Art of Performance: A Critical Anthology*, ed. Gregory Battcock and Robert Nickas, New York: E. P. Dutton, pp. 166–80.

Pavis, Patrice (1992) 'Theatre and the media: specificity and interference', in *Theatre at the Crossroads of Culture*, trans. Loren Kruger, London and New York: Routledge, pp. 99–135.

Phelan, Peggy (1993a) *Unmarked: The Politics of Performance*, London and New York: Routledge.

Phelan, Peggy (1993b) 'Preface: arresting performances of sexual and racial difference: toward a theory of performative film', *Women & Performance: A Journal of Feminist Theory* 6(2): 5–10.

Whitman, Willson (1937) *Bread and Circuses: A Study of Federal Theatre*, New York: Oxford University Press.

Some Cause[illegible]

An[illegible] trying to help a person with im[illegible] h[illegible] must ha[illegible]e accurate informatio[illegible] the t[illegible] of loss and how it has arisen. How an [illegible] such information will be d[illegible] The different types of [illegible] and some of the more co[illegible] that cause it are [illegible] h[illegible]. Some of the ways in which the extent [illegible] can be measured are outlined [illegible] and 4.

THE [illegible]ATURE OF [illegible] LOSS

A [illegible] may be placed [illegible] egories. Firstly there are [illegible] the o[illegible] and middle [illegible] lo[illegible] Secondly, there are condi[illegible] in[illegible], which give rise to [illegible] *[illegible] loss*. A third *type of loss*, [illegible] dealt with here. [illegible] such as bra[illegible] or abnorm[illegible] mental rather than physical in [illegible] central [illegible] sensor[illegible] aphasi[illegible] is una[illegible] the [illegible] although he has no difficulty [illegible] so[illegible] Fi[illegible] there is *[illegible]* which the [illegible] is partly conduct[illegible] neural. Apart from the tests [illegible] [illegible], it is possible to [illegible] whether an individua[illegible] tive or sens[illegible] signs:

[illegible] to a chronic [illegible] may be suppura-tive or non-[illegible] example of a non-[illegible] secretory [illegible] after an inflammatory [illegible] by antibiotics. The action [illegible] the infection but the fluid, [illegible] middle [illegible] and gradually [illegible] glue-like in consistency. [illegible] the more the movement of the [illegible] in the middle [illegible] is impede[illegible] If [illegible] hearing may deteriorate further [illegible] the [illegible], or the disrup-[illegible] the ossicular chain. [illegible] otitis media may occur [illegible] drum has become [illegible] providing an alternative to the [illegible] route by which infe[illegible] may [illegible] It is for this reason that [illegible] with a perforated ear-drum is generally [illegible] The fluid discharged through [illegible] either odourless or foul smelling. [illegible] important, for while [illegible] [illegible] as relatively harmless, the latter [illegible] of a potentially serious [illegible] as [illegible] of the middle [illegible] contains [illegible] which may destroy the [illegible] If untreated the [illegible] grows insidiously and [illegible] invade the [illegible], changing a treatable con-[illegible] impairment into an irreversible sen-[illegible].

	[illegible]	[illegible]URAL LO[illegible]
TYPICAL SPEECH	[illegible] his [illegible] conduction	[illegible] and with a tendency [illegible] as the person has difficulty in hearing [illegible] voice

[illegible]

[illegible] bone. [illegible] engim[illegible] [illegible] sclerosis [illegible] noticed by people [illegible] twenties although [illegible] about thirty years [illegible] the stapes becom[illegible] oval window becau[illegible] spongy bone. At first [illegible] although hearing acu[illegible] rates. (There may even [illegible] gets no worse.) In its lat[illegible] invade the [illegible] that [illegible] from a conductive [illegible] a mixed [illegible] [illegible] shows the general indicat[illegible] impairment described earlier in this chapter. It also has the following characteristics:

- It is estimated to be twice as prevalent in women as in men; pregnancy [illegible] itating factor.
- There is usually, though not necessarily, a family history of [illegible].
- [illegible] conductive [illegible], bone conduction will be better than [illegible] conduction; it may be possible to hear [illegible] one even [illegible] there is difficulty [illegible] normal speech.
- Tinnitus is often pre[illegible] in mild cases may be the most distressing symptom.
- The [illegible] loss usually begins in one ear and then [illegible] becomes bilateral, but the degree of hearing loss is not the same in both ears.
- [illegible] is more prevalent [illegible] than in [illegible] among the fair-[illegible]

While otitis media and otosclerosis are the two most [illegible] conductive impairment they a[illegible] media is a disease [illegible] its consequences may persist [illegible] otosclerosis becomes apparent in ear[illegible] The [illegible] tary [illegible] that can [illegible] sis [illegible] does not arise in [illegible] there are [illegible] differences that can be deter[illegible] the [illegible] in otitis media both the [illegible] and the [illegible] tube show signs of abnormality, in [illegible] they are usually normal.

[illegible] NEURAL HEARING

[illegible] loss may occur at any stage of [illegible] associated with birth and with [illegible] degenerative consequences of ageing. Con[illegible] is outside the scope of this book, but among [illegible] causes of profound hearing loss at or [illegible] are the mother contracting rubella – German measles – during the first three months of [illegible] rhesus incompatibility and anoxia, or lack [illegible] causing [illegible] damage at the [illegible] adulthood or middle age [illegible] disease [illegible] expectation [illegible] usually accompanied by some [illegible]

[illegible] Whatever [illegible] vertigo [illegible] which usually [illegible], is the [illegible] usually takes the [illegible] in which the affected [illegible] he or his surroundings are [illegible] may also take the [illegible] down or, [illegible] the bridge of a [illegible]

THURS 20th FEB → FRIDAY 21st FEB

Staff : EN – [redacted] & [redacted]

ON – [redacted]

EM –

Volunteers : EN – [redacted], [redacted], [redacted]

ON – [redacted] [redacted]

EM – NONE

Laundrette : OK 6.00pm, 6-15pm, 6-30pm to 6-45pm. People were hanging around outside the shelter, no probs.

[redacted] Off his head on entering, as was [redacted]. may be clucking. Fairly quiet start apart from [redacted] they both settled down at 9-30pm.

NEEDLE Found in lounge, capped, where [redacted] had been lying down watchin TV. It was unused, no fuss made since I seem to have been the only one to spot it.

[redacted] & [redacted] Have been thrown out of [redacted] length of ban not known. They arrived here at 11-30 following advanced warning from [redacted] You lucky people you.

[redacted] 1 RANITIDINE TAB 1.10 AM.

3 AM NEW FACE. [redacted] 26 YEARS OLD, TALL WITH SHORT DARK HAIR. HAS SPENT MOST OF LAST YEAR IN [redacted] IS ON MEDICATION (PROCYCLIDINE). HE SAYS THAT HE WAS GIVEN SOME TABLETS LAST WEEK (STRONG SCHIZOPHRENIA DRUGS) WHICH HE RESPONDED BADLY TO AND SO IS NOT TAKING ANY MORE – HE SAYS HE WAS GIVEN THEM BY ACCIDENT – FOR FLU! HE SEEMS FINE, WELL IN CONTROL NO EVIDENCE OF PROBLEMS – HAD A VERY NORMAL CHAT WITH HIM. HAS BEEN STAYING AT HIS SISTERS IN [redacted] SAID HIS MOTHER WAS NOT WELL RECEIVING SOME KIND OF FREQUENT INJECTIONS (NOT SURE WHAT FOR). HE DOESN'T FEEL ABLE SPEND TIME WITH HER BECAUSE OF HIS STEPFATHER. HE INTENDS GETTING A BEDSIT IN [redacted]

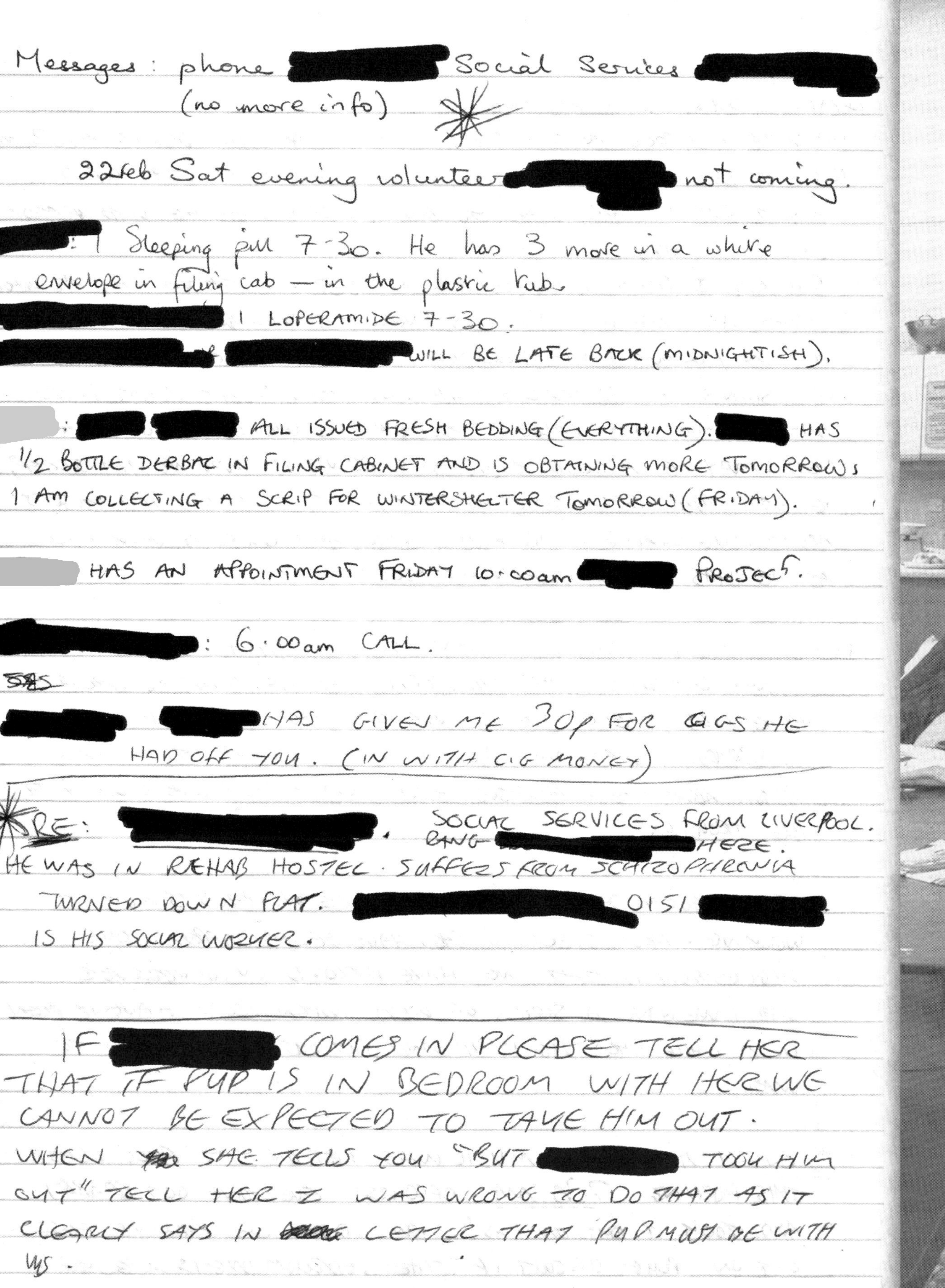

Messages: phone Social Services
(no more info)

22 feb Sat evening volunteer not coming.

: 1 Sleeping pill 7-30. He has 3 more in a white envelope in filing cab — in the plastic tub.

1 LOPERAMIDE 7-30.

& WILL BE LATE BACK (MIDNIGHTISH).

: ALL ISSUED FRESH BEDDING (EVERYTHING). HAS 1/2 BOTTLE DERBAC IN FILING CABINET AND IS OBTAINING MORE TOMORROW. I AM COLLECTING A SCRIP FOR WINTERSHELTER TOMORROW (FRIDAY).

HAS AN APPOINTMENT FRIDAY 10·00am PROJECT.

: 6·00am CALL.

HAS GIVEN ME 30p FOR CIGS HE HAD OFF YOU. (IN WITH CIG MONEY)

RE: . SOCIAL SERVICES FROM LIVERPOOL. RANG HERE. HE WAS IN REHAB HOSTEL. SUFFERS FROM SCHIZOPHRENIA TURNED DOWN FLAT. 0151 IS HIS SOCIAL WORKER.

IF COMES IN PLEASE TELL HER THAT IF PUP IS IN BEDROOM WITH HER WE CANNOT BE EXPECTED TO TAKE HIM OUT. WHEN SHE TELLS YOU "BUT TOOK HIM OUT" TELL HER I WAS WRONG TO DO THAT AS IT CLEARLY SAYS IN LETTER THAT PUP MUST BE WITH US.

The *Oresteia* of the Socìetas Raffaello Sanzio

Valentina Valentini

The Socìetas Raffello Sanzio was founded in 1981 by Romeo and Claudia Castelluci, Paolo and Chiara Guidi. Under the direction of Romeo Castellucci the ensemble established a theatre school in 1988 (the Theatrical School of Descent) and a publishing house in Cesena where since 1995 their working place and site for public happenings has been the Comandini Theatre, an old mechanical school restored by the Socìetas. Amongst their many radical productions, they have shown work at the Venice Biennale – *La Generalissima* (1984); Documenta VIII – *I Miserabili* (1987); Weiner Festwochen – *Amleto* (1992); and Theater der Welt – *Oresteia* (1996).

The Socìetas Raffaello Sanzio, before turning its attention to classical texts such as *Hamlet* and the *Oresteia*, staged a rich repertory of myths belonging to non-western traditions. Out of these traditions it drew fable-like plots and a universe in which the human and the divine, the world of the living and that of the after-life, animals and monsters all appeared on the stage, establishing a distance from the world of the spectator. Such theatre, wielding its 'pre-linguistic arguments' as weapons, aimed at overwhelming and surprising the audience with vision, thus compelling the spectator to abandon the intellectual game of 'debating over the meaning'. The spectator was left exposed to 'being struck by lightning'.

The Socìetas Raffaello Sanzio demonstrates this mythopoeic tendency not only in works based on traces of mythical stories (such as *La discesa di Inanna* which narrates the struggle of the goddess of love, and the war to take possession of the kingdom of the dead). In fact, it is a tendency founded on the intention of creating 'drama', of creating a timeless theatre, 'walled-in and immobile', eternal as an inscription on a tombstone (C. and R. Castellucci 1992: 102). Therefore, both the more theatrically 'political' works, such as *Santa Sofia* (1985) and *I Miserabili* (1986), and the more mythical-legendary ones, such as *La discesa di Inanna* (1989) and *Gilgamesh* (1990), aim to establish a realm of the imaginary and a ritual praxis which allows no involvement with phenomenological reality. To draw from myth to fuel one's own mythological production implies the creation of a theatrical world composed of archetypal and anti-historic images: agricultural myths of birth and death, of fertility, which merge with the psychoanalytic/archaeological realm of the imaginary. Their basic political value derives from the re-establishment of language around the 'figure of diversity' (i.e. the wretched/ ignorant), on the materialism of the theatre set and on the supremacy of the gaze. It emerges feeding a tension between the word and the body, conceiving of the theatrical event like a voyage of initiation from the shadows to the light, like an act of epiphany.

Because of this 'religious' (conjunctive) vision of the theatrical act as an organism formed by the unity of (masculine) language and (feminine) prelogical expressive matter, the performances of the Socìetas Raffaello Sanzio are not self-reflective,

Performance Research 2(3), pp.58-64 © Routledge 1997

despite having the theatre as their centre of speculation. The theatrical event does not represent a theatre-world (utopian, possible, current or past), but rather expects to create one in its separation and difference ('il Teatro dei Murati' or 'the barricaded theatre'). This is possible because language, having an originating force of its own, undertakes a performative role: they say that to have something done, words are as good as things. The theatrical event is not required to describe the world, but rather to re-create it through the prodigious power of the voice, a voice liberated from the gesture and uncompromised by the ostentatious display on stage, one with its means of expression: the mouth, the palate, the tongue. Words and actions live separately from one another, excluding one another, rather than integrating themselves as has been so far asserted and practised by the company.

Such poetics follow in the wake of the thought of Antonin Artaud, in that twentieth-century theatrical tradition which outlaws all subjectivity with its memorial and autobiographic declinations and excludes enslavement to the daily chronicle. In this outlook, mythopoeic thought and ritualistic practice strive to achieve the same objective: to found a 'necessary theatre' whose materialistic basis is in the first place the actor, emerging as an 'abode' for the text. In this way, 'body is inhabited by the true word: that of the material body an origin' (C. and R. Castellucci 1992: 108). Thus, if the voice must express the physicality of the words (chosen for their rhythm, their tone, their sound), it must take on substance and density, filling itself with that slimy matter of which the body is composed. From the depths of the body, where it resides in the 'recesses of the belly', the voice rises up into the throat.

In terms of the tradition of Artaudian thought, the Socìetas Raffaello Sanzio engages that which is closest to performance art, which in its own way had produced a strong realm of the imaginary around the power of the body, the sole source of truth and self-consciousness: an abused body, subject to forces, dangers, tensions and risks.

The actor in the company is the victim required to celebrate the ritual of degradation and regeneration of the performance-event. Its (unreachable) goal is that of animal stupidity, inarticulate expressiveness, the equivalent of the critical asphyxia that is the ideal state of the spectator. In fact, as in fables, the stage of the Socìetas Raffaello Sanzio's works is occupied to an equal degree by actors, animals and things, each with a role as active subject, regardless of its living or inert state. The presence of animals on the stage (white baboons, snakes, dogs . . .), since the work *Alla Bellezza tanto antica* (1987), constitutes a tense challenge to the presence on set of the actor, glorifying rather than degrading him or her. The attributes of the actors in the theatre-world of the Socìetas Raffaello Sanzio, in addition to reaching an animalistic pre-expressiveness, stoop to become an obstructive body, immobile and mute. A recurrent action in

• **Hermes in *Oresteia*, Socìetas Raffaello Sanzio, 1995. Photo: SRS, Cesena**

their performance has the actor close up all his or her orifices, shutting off all perceptive channels, in a kind of self-punishment, not only because the mask is physically painful but above all because it leads to the darkness of not seeing, the silence of not speaking. On the positive side, the cutting off of all channels of communication between the world and oneself becomes a ritual of purification, as in that solitary, ascetic practice of icon-makers, who, prior to setting about the painting of the icon, underwent a sort of 'fasting of the eyes'. The mute, immobile actor operates on the same principle, with the role of silencing the Babel of voices and restoring a condition of listening to and pronouncement of the word after its purification. Immobility is a measure of time: it is the figure of the Herald rigid at the centre of the stage for the entire duration of the work *I Miserabili,* 'degree zero of time, degree zero of the act, degree zero of place' (C. Castellucci 1992: 86), the sleep of Hamlet, Clytemnestra's reclining. Both of these figures of deprival are, however, ready to reverse roles to become the opposite: a womb in which, once inseminated, the still-invisible theatrical event matures. It is a mythology of the double, of parallel rhythm of destruction and creation, of disappearance and appearance, of masculine and feminine principles, of form and matter, dark and light, silence and voices.

It is a dualism that does not imply elimination; it is not a dialectical principle in which the contrasts resolve themselves, but rather a polarity of opposites which continue to coexist. According to Nietzsche's scheme, the tragic is the battlefield for antitheses, resulting in neither conciliation nor redemption. There is no dialectic in the tragic because unity does not arise from the contradictions; there is only infinite contrast devoid of *telos*.

FROM EASTERN MYTH TO WESTERN BOOK

A span of almost ten years reaches from the figure of the 'barricaded theatre' (1987), a metaphor in which the Socìetas Raffaello Sanzio's 'iconoclastic' theatrical ethics and aesthetics were condensed, through the cycle of works dedicated to the (Mesopotamian and Egyptian) myths, to the two most recent productions of *Amleto, la veemente esteriorita della morte di un mollusco* ('Hamlet, the vehement outwardness of the death of a mollusc') (1992b) and the *Oresteia* (1995), which represent a sort of caving-in to the book and the writing. This most recent confrontation with the great tragic works of the history of theatre, the Socìetas Raffaello Sanzio contends, was certainly not driven by the desire to 'return to the order of the grand tradition'. In fact, *Amleto* . . . causes one to forget entirely the Shakespearean tragedy since the text is taken as a 'crossroads at which to contemplate the myth of the actor': an actor suffering from autism perennially clings to his stuffed animal and punishes himself for his guilt in the 'shameful conduct of his mother' (a metaphor for the Theatre). It is a work about the relationship between actor, author and set: where 'for the actor, the author plays the role of a father and the set that of an (incestuous) mother' (R. Castellucci 1992b).

The operation of the stripping of the theatre, begun ten years earlier, in this work becomes a sadistic decimation of the dramaturgical apparatus. The *fabula* (plot) being completely excluded, time consists in that which fills in the pauses, the interruptions, the repetitions and unchanging state (the only action permitted is sleep).

The word in *Amleto* . . . is not spoken; there are gestural sounds and the occasional sentence thrown out like some meteor through outer space. The depth of silence, a silence of total immersion in an autistic world, is accentuated by the repeated gunfire which accosts the surprised spectator, frightening the audience. *Amleto* . . . in the history of the Socìetas Raffaello Sanzio indicates the fulfilment of the actor's task through the passage of the disease (autism). The disjunction of 'to be, or not to be' is transformed, through the conjunction 'and', into the movement between death and sleep. In this perspective, the adoption of the Shakespearean tragedy did not result in the denial of its own theatrical cosmogony. It might even have marked an extension beyond the tragic dualism and the immersion in a world devoid of difference, of contrast and of colours, a world where animals are not set against the *logos*, nor the masculine against the feminine, nor nature against culture.

In the essay 'Teatro dei Murati' (1987) Claudia Castellucci claimed that theatre should seek its sources outside of Europe and North America, and that Giotto, Leonardo and Picasso were only of relative greatness, when considered from non-western points of view. In *Amleto . . .*, this recommendation finds its most radical application; the Shakespearean tragedy is literally uprooted from history, from theatre, from culture . . .

What happens with the *Oresteia*, a work which inscribes in myth the passage and dominion of civilization over barbarism? Having reached the far limits with *Amleto . . .*, is this a return to the origins of western civilization? To answer this, it is necessary to look at the work, trying to understand the way in which the classical myth, with all of the various interpretive layers imposed on it, has engaged with the mythical universe of the Socìetas Raffaello Sanzio examined so far.

• Orestes in *Oresteia*, Socìetas Raffaello Sanzio, 1995. Photo: SRS, Cesena

The work is based on the pattern of the double: *Obscuritas* and *claritas*, the plump bodies of Clytemnestra and Cassandra and the emaciated ones of the ephebic adolescents (Orestes and Pylades); the milk and the blood (which mix in Clytemnestra's dream when her breast is bitten by a viper); the wet and the dry, the struggle between *logos* (Athens and Apollo defending Orestes) and *soma* (Clytemnestra and the Choephori who persecute him), On the stage, these contrasts are made visible through, on one side, the figure of Clytemnestra who establishes the series Theatre, Body, mother, Whale, cavity-belly, blood-excrement, and in contrast on the other side, the adolescent autism of Orestes and Pylades who compose an opposite series with the dryness and whiteness of powder and sand, cutting off breath and bringing death.

In addition to this binary opposition, two functions operate simultaneously in the work: *disjunction* and *conjunction*. On the one hand the blood-spewing body of Clytemnestra, in the series of the organism, and on the other the 'mechanism' formed of various pieces of motorized apparatus (pistons, pipes, batteries . . .) called upon to activate both inanimate objects (such as the rabbit statues that constitute the chorus) and people (the pneumatic arm which Pylades grafts on to the body of Orestes in order to kill his mother, etc.). Each of these two series is both disjoined from and joined with the other; even the organism breathes and feeds through prostheses which, in turn, have lives of their own. Having committed the murder of his mother, Orestes removes his pneumatic arm which conserves the movement undergone when it was attached to his body: conjunction and disjunction. Likewise Agamemnon's throne – a revolving chair – continues to move even after being vacated by the body of the murdered king. After the disruption of equilibrium following the violent deaths, and the change in the dynamic relationship among 'actors' (understood both as organisms with their real kinetic energy and mechanisms with their virtual kinetic energy), the stage-world attempts to restore the original conditions. That is why the mechanisms take on the kinetic energy lost by the death of the living organism, thus preventing its dissipation.

An exchange of energy thus takes place between the two series, with their reciprocal functions remaining unaltered. The organism and the mechanism are united along a line of conjunction (a spark, a discharge, the 'and' of Hamlet) which controls the exchange and raises the power of their contrasting nature. It is the aimless turning of the empty throne which screams of the violence suffered by the organism. The mechanisms are integrated as 'actors' on the set, part of the company's *caravanserai,* on an equal footing with the animals and the bodies of the actors. Their presence indicates neither the difference between nature and culture, nor the reduction of the set-world to a still life; rather it is a more realistic integration and interchange between the organic and the mechanical. It is the 'cyberbody' of Stelarc conceived as an 'engineered object'.

The work overturns the accepted reading of the text: in Aeschylus's text the Erinyes are 'wild and blood-thirsty divinities', who 'transform themselves into the protectors of vegetation, of cultivation and breeding, passing from the vocabulary of the hunt to that of agriculture' (Vidal-Naquet in Vernant and Vidal-Naquet 1976: 144). This does not lead in linear fashion to the elimination of the wild, of the beastly; these qualities are merely destined to battle it out beyond the city walls, in wars and not between brothers. In the performance the characters representing the *polis*, such as the chorus, are emblems of vileness (literally taking the form of rabbits). In contrast, the carnal nature of the mother series stands out, thus affirming the supremacy of natural right in the face of the new laws instituted by Athens and Apollo with the court of the Areopagus. Clytemnestra is 'the abyssal creature who pulls all things into the depths', the whale-woman inspired by Melville's *Moby Dick*

• The Choephori in *Oresteia*. Socìetas Raffaello Sanzio, 1995. Photo: SRS, Cesena

(Socìetas Raffaello Sanzio 1995). The Agamemnon of Aeschylus's text, but also Orestes himself, is both the 'hunter and the hunted', the lion and the eagle, sly predatory animal (the snake and the wolf). Yet at the same time he is an animal caught in a trap, 'victim of the lioness Clytemnestra and the cowardly lion Aegisthus', shown in the work as a violent, infantile torturer who enjoys dressing up as king in the royal cloak and crown. The role of Agamemnon is played by a Downs Syndrome actor who laughs, dances and sings, which is not to imply a negation or degradation of the image of the valiant and astute warrior.

The pathological characters in the Socìetas Raffaello Sanzio's *Oresteia* are Orestes and Electra. The latter (described in the text with wolf-like attributes) is shown as having reverted to, or perhaps never having outgrown, the oral stage; she sucks on her brother's shoe, isolated in an autistic

• Agamemnon in *Oresteia*. Socìetas Raffaello Sanzio, 1995. Photo: SRS, Cesena

world in which she attributes living qualities to inanimate objects. Her brother Orestes is represented in the text as a double figure: simultaneously innocent and guilty, bringing disaster and salvation (vindicating his father's murder). But above all, according to Vidal-Naquet, his is the duplicity of adolescence: 'he is the ephebic apprentice-man and apprentice-warrior' (Vidal-Naquet in Vernant and Vidal-Naquet 1976: 138). The Orestes of the Socìetas Raffaello Sanzio, along with his alter-ego Pylades, is an unsettling figure with his white body and the mask of a clown; he is neither tragic nor comic. The figures which populate the set of the *Oresteia* form a tribe of numbed, stupefied ephebes, metaphor-bodies, autistics. Although bearing the names of the characters of the tragedy, they have nothing in common with them.

The Socìetas Raffaello Sanzio's *Oresteia* is a work impregnated with the sentiments of the tragic, yet it is not a tragedy. The tragic hero's obsessive pursuit of truth is absent, neither represented nor demonstrated through actions. The violence which the *dramatis personae* undergo or enact cannot be classified as pure or impure, holy or profane, and neither can the subsequent guilt or punishment. Though conceived as doubles, the characters engage in no dialogues. In the passages which distinguish the tragic hero, the work plays up his isolation, his distancing, timelessness and placelessness, a stranger even to himself (Cassandra is enclosed in a glass case). This indicates a dislocation of the tragedy from a semantic level to a level of expressive material. The task of expressing the pathos of the events of the tragedy is assigned to sound, as in the earth-shaking crash which follows the killing of Clytemnestra. Sound is the element that creates tension, terror, discomfort and a sense of the unbearable. On the other hand lies the plot of silence: the tragedy of self-silencing and solipsism. Sound intervenes not suddenly, as in *Amleto . . .*, but through the creation of a persistent state, like a closely knit fabric, a hard glaze merging mechanical, electronic and corporal sounds (voices, sighs, groans, hiccups).

THE MYTH: HOW TO ESCAPE THE POWER OF THEATRE

Let us return to the question posed above: the relationship between the Socìetas Raffaello Sanzio's classical works (such as the *Oresteia*) and their theatrical mythology. As a distancing measure, we can direct the question to a contemporary Italian author (writer, theatrical and cinematographic director) who has dealt with the question of myth in a radical manner: Carmelo Bene.

To render 'minor' a classical text which is itself 'major': that is the attitude of Carmelo Bene in the face of Shakespearean tragedies (*Romeo and Juliet, Richard III, Macbeth*, etc.) . This operation of 'lessening' of the text is in the first place a mutilation, a stripping, a rewriting in which the plot can no longer be recognized and the characters are overrun by their literary identity and their dramatic function to the point of being absorbed by the sole 'operator' present on the set, like a demiurge conducting the 'concerto for solo actor', the orchestration of the voices and sound through which Carmelo Bene strips the Shakespearean world down to itself, having incorporated it. This is the means of escaping from the power of the theatre as institution, from the rule of plot, of character, of the coherence of representation, from everything which might be transformed into a stabilizing element. The classical myth destabilized by Carmelo Bene's stage act, which involves continual variation, becomes a sort of formula for the Dionysian ritual of unhinging theatrical representation, wavering between the heroic and the pathetic, the sublime and the parody, the child's game and metaphysical chess. From this viewpoint, and according to the reading of Gilles Deleuze, Carmelo Bene's theatrical production traces a "figure of minority conscience latent in everyone' (Bene and Deleuze 1978: 90), indicating, that is, the route to escape from the tyranny of history, of culture, of language and from the normalization of the judicious gesture and of the completed action. The precondition necessary for art to act politically is that 'the variation never ceases to vary'. that the movement of unhinging and disintegration holds its own in the face of the equally strong pressure to re-establish a new order (new myths, new worlds . . .). In the *Oresteia* of the Socìetas Raffaello Sanzio, the classical text is stripped down in its descriptions and in the tales of the chorus as well as in its dialogues, so that on the one hand the spoken lines press closely upon the actions to which they refer, and on the other they leave space for the scene to unfold wordlessly. The process is a double one: the text is emptied with relation to the staging, which works towards a loss of sense, but simultaneously the text, an archeological fragment, is preserved as evidence of the myth. According to the first assumption, the text is a cultural source, a paper apparatus, which, at a certain point in the process of staging, must be forgotten. 'No reading the *Oresteia*' was the restriction placed on the actors. Regarding the second, the *Oresteia* respects the temporal sequence of the *fabula*, is the relationship between the text and the actions on stage, between what the characters say and what they do; in this way the plastic and chromatic apparatus of images plays a role of visual metaphor with respect to the literary text. This consistency between the actual representation and the text which manipulates it sets aside (at least temporarily) the vanishing point, the imbalance, the dissonant unity that is the threshold on which the 'minority conscience of theatre' is contested. The *Oresteia* might thus place itself as the latest in the movement in which modern Italian theatre (from George Strehler to Luca Ronconi) was reborn after the Second World War, the tradition of director's theatre.

Translated by Tom Rankin

REFERENCES

Bene, Carmelo and Deleuze, Gilles (1978) 'Un manifesto di meno', in *Sovrapposizioni,* Milan: Feltrinelli.

Castelluci, Claudia and Castelluci, Romeo (1992) *Il Teatro della Socìetas Raffaello Sanzio*, Milan: Ubulibri.

——(1992b) Socìetas Raffaello Sanzio *Amleto* (programma di sala), Weiner Festwochen Big/ Motion, Vienna, 16–18 May.

Socìetas Raffaello Sanzio (1995) *Orestea (una tragedia organica?),* Cesena: SRS.

Vernant, Jean Pierre and Vidal-Naquet, Pierre (1976 [1972]) *Mythe et Tragédie en Grèce ancienne*, Paris: Librairie François Maspero.

No Hiding Place

Alan Read

I have a childhood recollection of a television programme on a small black-and-white screen in the corner of a room in the early 1960s. A man, the fugitive, was running from bus station to back alley, evading capture, and on the run righting the injustice that had been done to him. Like all good cliffhangers, time and space were intimately bound. The fugitive's face was a pale reflection of his troubled past and foreclosed future, his proximity to a receding hope of justice. The time of his freedom was running out as the FBI closed in, while the space of his endeavour was systematically shut down from first one side then the other. The fugitive's eyes were in a constant state of motion, taking in peripheral movement to left and right. The time of the programme ticked away, dénouement was inevitable but always to be suspended.

I am sure this was a Sunday evening when another time of freedom ticked away: the end of the weekend. These were the days of a new import to Britain, the game show: *Sunday Night at the London Palladium* with its uncannily magnified clock followed by *Double Your Money* and *Take Your Pick*. Each show counted down the seconds on another contestant's hopes of winning an exotic holiday, or a grinning MC counted out the chance of luxuriating in a new three-piece suite.

• David Janssen, *The Fugitive*. Photo: The Vintage Magazine Co. Archive.

Was I dreaming that, once upon a time and far away, time and space were whole? And that here was a crossroads, where domestic space and travel were to be desired, won, or, for the first time, bought by those who wished to circumvent the luck of the lucky? Crime and punishment were scheduled to mix with good fortune, escape from the clutches of the law coincided with the chance to win a flight to exotica on an island, or, better still, to take possession of a quality settee and luxuriate in the privacy of one's own home.

Now, on a smaller screen in another corner, in colour, and sometimes on a Sunday, the genres are mixed with the fugitive being pursued by the telemedia – as the surveillance cameras of *Police Camera Action* infra-red a darting figure way below, or Anneka Rice is run to ground 'just in time'. Winners take all and losers are banged up, deluged by telephonic grassers. The domestic and the exotic are all the same now, been there, done that, the hunt and the money are all that's left.

The time and space of suspense have come apart with nowhere left to run to and all the time in the world to do it in. Where would the fugitive find refuge now? Justice depended on the time that passed under cover. No hiding-place, no justice.

The intensive mapping that has forced the fugitive into the open, which characterizes the last two decades, is fundamentally different from the ordnance of the previous two hundred. Surveying the street from the air, ordnance has lost control of

Performance Research 2(3), pp.65-74 © Routledge 1997

the delinquent – a satellite shot of the hot spots of the city is no substitute for 'the beat' where law enforcement began at the time of street lighting by knowing the attraction of hidden trapdoors to subterranean cellars, ditches and tunnels, back alleys and connecting passageways. Crowd control has substituted the chase, the city has in Paul Virilio's term been 'overexposed' (Virilio 1993).

I suspect the fugitive now has nowhere to go but time to kill. The space of the discreet and hidden has been turned inside out by a series of economic, political and legislative assaults, leaving an exhausted landscape as fair game to be worked over by cultural historians, semioticians and geographers. The wastes that are left, the remainder they are working, is a rich one, but nevertheless an increasingly aestheticized one – just on the margins of the sites where a fugitive might properly seek to right wrongs and secure justice. Performance could, if it wished and was in the right hands, lead us back towards that space of justice or simply decorate that space to make the fugitive's last hours a bit more comfortable and pleasing on the eye. Decoration would seem to hold sway in the late 1990s; something deeper would require alliances with those who 'know space', who have spent some time not taking it for granted. In order to understand how best to deepen the terms of engagement this would seem an apposite time to seek another rapprochement between forms of practice and theory.

The discourses of space, built form and urban context have become the pre-eminent critical idiom at the end of the twentieth century. Sensitive to questions of community readdressed in new and radical languages, artists, theoreticians, social scientists and those within and beyond the architectural profession reach for the strategies and structures of the populated street to articulate the sense of their work. To be spaced out is no longer to be depleted, as Terry Eagleton recently remarked in the *London Review of Books*.

The attractions and invigorations of spatial critique would seem to have opened up an arena for affirmative, politicized discourse. But what should be noted at the outset about these languages is how they are predominantly conducted by men, how insensitive to race and the realities of the urban everyday they can be, and how unacquainted they are with the diverse discourses of the performative and theatre's long-term engagement with community. Here, what Judith Butler has called the 'merely cultural' relegates the potential relationship between theatre knowledges and experiences below the more significant work of economic and political analysis instead of drawing the two closer together for the purpose of a fuller understanding of the street itself and what takes place there.

This is a particular loss for theory. And given that any loss for critical discourse will be reciprocally felt in amplified measure and in the long term by practice, a loss for performance. Ironically it is the cultural, within the performance arena, with its natural terrain of complex associations between levels of political and artistic discourse, that provides a corollary to the simplifications of current spatial discussion. The appeals made by those within this debate not to forget space as a dynamic of social relations, space as gendered territory, space not as stasis but the ground for action and politics, are bountifully answered by the complex operations of performance through space and time.

For instance, the exemplary performance work in Britain of groups such as Platform and the duo Forster and Heighes exemplifies performance within a spatial moment precisely resisting classification. Platform's truly durational research and installation practice reforge concealed histories of geographical and global markets. In their 1990s project *Homeland* Platform mixed social science research, practical experimentation, installation and performance to interrogate the Londoner's conception of home while inviting the capital to consider its part within a wider European homeland. Through the conceptual link of light, its practical manifestation in the light-bulb, and the search for its source in electric power, Platform traversed a copper mine in Portugal, a coal mine in South Wales and a sand quarry in Hungary, via three institutional conglomerates who control power to the light switch: General Electric, British Coal and Rio Tinto Zinc. This pan-European and international enquiry was then reimagined within a mobile installation that moved across London, stopping at significant junctions to embrace the perceptions and experiences of an audience reconfigured as participatory research subjects. I recall drawing my idea of home on to a small piece of paper and seeing it clipped up with hundreds of others.

The intimate Anglo-Saxon acts of historical recovery that Forster and Heighes conduct in 'principled' buildings such as Union Chapel or the Mary Ward Centre in London would appear to be as distanced from the global complexities of Platform as one might imagine. Yet as Gaston Bachelard remarked, the simple is only ever the complex simplified, and it is this resistance to reduction that characterizes their work. *Preliminary Hearing,* produced as part of the 1997 London International Festival of Theatre, continued their archeological excavation of the ethical foundations of architecture, the hidden moralities that shaped London's meeting-places and congregational centres. In the case of the recovery of the story of Mary Ward House, a series of lectures, demonstrations, installations and site constructions revealed the historical components of modern welfare provision, school meals, nursery education and care for people with disabilities. I recall being inundated by Morris dancers, white working men, dancing gently together in public.

More recently in London in June and July 1997 acts such as Neil Bartlett's *The Seven Sacraments of Nicolas Poussin* at the Royal London Hospital or Enrique Vargas's *Oraculos* in a King's Cross depot are intermediary projects, in the fullest sense of that term, which carry echoes of the site specific while resisting the urge to embrace the locality on any other level than as 'backdrop'. Each takes a spatial configuration, the hospital in one, the labyrinth in the other, and sets it off against another pictorial space, the paintings of Poussin and the Tarot, to open up an interface for narrative exploration. They are none the less potentially peripatetic: Whitechapel and the Royal London Hospital could become London Bridge and Guy's Hospital, the King's Cross depot could (and was at one time meant to) become the Camden Roundhouse. These are significant projects as they are the umbilical link between the highly conscious and self-reflexive location of the former projects and another much more familiar genre, that is, performance that situates itself in the terrain marked theatre. Around this spectrum of work ranging from the culturally rooted to the displaced are the interventions within localities; I am thinking here of groups such as Entelechy in south-east London, who would be surprised at any privileging of the discourses of space, knowing that their wellspring is an auratic sensibility to neighbourhood, the particular time and place of their action.

While theoreticians such as Marc Augé (1995), Beatriz Colomina (1995) and Doreen Massey (1994) have recognized the critical significance of in-between space, liminal spaces and threshold sites, particularly with regard to questions of identity, gender and domestic/public worlds, performance has of course met its stauncher allies in the last decade in a fertile terrain of writers, film-makers and artists whose disposition has been to get down there, not it would seem in any archaic oppositional sense, but rather through relational practices to sites.

I will come to the pre-eminent foot-soldier, the writer Iain Sinclair, in a while, but it should be noted here that Patrick Keiller in films such as *London* and *Robinson in Space* has taken the art of walking, then waiting, to an ultimate moment. As Sinclair says about his colleague's work: 'Keiller's separate takes (different angles, lenses, distances) on the same subject are a way of articulating space.' Keiller's work was picked up as a reference point in my private discussion with the visual artists Cornford and Cross, at the Institute of Contemporary Arts, London, on 17 July 1997. Installations by Cornford and Cross, such as *Camelot* in Stoke-on-Trent and *New Holland* in Norwich, display another kind of relational awareness. In

Stoke 100 m of security fencing 3 m high was placed around three neglected grass verges, drawing out an array of ambivalence and anger from those who thought they knew their town, while in Norwich a steel barn was placed adjacent to the Sainsbury Centre for Visual Arts simultaneously evoking a 'Bernard Matthews' turkey-breeder unit while playing off Norman Foster's technocratic architecture and emitting a continuous soundtrack of house and garage music.

Both artists work with a sense of the temporary, avoiding institutionalization at every turn. Their point of beginning is a discussion of ideas and a conceptual response to place, making the space they are working on reveal itself. There is no audience in mind for this work; they may be drawing out dimensions of place but they do not claim to unmask ideological conditions. Their politics, like those of Iain Sinclair perhaps, are manifested by wishing things a bit too far, to let something run on unchecked and to see what will happen. They ask: 'What happens if we take a leap rather than an incremental step?' In *Camelot* the question of space is conducted through an encroachment on wilderness, with the act of privatization and sectioning of space conducted as an operation of protection. For Cornford and Cross pedestrianism is a necessity as well as an aesthetic choice, they work without a studio, distrusting the inhibition of scale such spaces induce, valuing the basic relationship between body and space, the relations between pacing and direct physical experience. Each of their works has to be circumvented on foot and draws out surprising affiliations with the work of formalists such as Carl André and Richard Serra.

• *Camelot*, Cornford and Cross, Stoke-on-Trent, 1996

In the work of Keiller as well as Cornford and Cross it is interesting to hear the under-commentary to practice that theoretical frameworks provide. Keiller's score for *Robinson in Space* incorporates a myriad voices and quotations musing on the spaces he traverses while Cornford and Cross effortlessly implicate and parody at least twenty years of public art discourses in their laconic dialogues with institutional brutalism. Theory here has mutated to the point of a set of associations and variations that each artist reconfigures, dissimulating between the space of the material and the mental.

But how far do these relational projects take us with regard to questions of politics and justice? Is the loss of the oppositional for the relational necessarily a forfeiting of contested ground? Since writing *Theatre and Everyday Life* (1993), in which spatial critique was a central concern, I have become increasingly aware of the elision of politics in the spatial turn. My concern had been to restore the plenitude of the empty space and to confront theatre with the implications of its predecessors. To recognize the precedent of location had explicit political and ethical imperatives: the purpose of the critique was to reveal ways in which theatre operates in antagonism to official views of reality. The aestheticization of space has now, ironically, occluded the transparency of events that once occurred there, and without time or historical perspective has jeopardized the meanings that might otherwise have been drawn from actions.

The deconstruction and distribution of the Berlin Wall as a public art object has become its significance; over Baghdad the celebration of anti-aircraft flak becomes a pyrotechnician's dream; the valorization of Swampy and the Eco warriors protesting at the tarmacking of England's 'green and pleasant land' is predicated on their expertise as subterranean designers; the return of Hong Kong to China sparks a debate about the decibel level of an eve-of-handover Elton John concert or the aesthetics of post-colonial nautical departure. Berlin, Manchester, Hong Kong, an international club circuit with each location divested of all but its banal associations. And the banal, which in French parlance once described the ovens used communally for baking, is precisely the least common gathering-point for concerted action or assertive remembrance.

While activism has retreated from the public realm it has regrouped around less localized and more transnational objectives. A historic association with protest and place has been superseded by global affiliations and space. *Pride* in London and Sydney, *Carnival* in Jamaica and Koln, *Feminism* in Beijing and New York, *Ecology* in Rio and Amsterdam. Here the site of action is displaced by the network of affiliation. But these political shifts are simultaneous with a harsher, faster proliferation of networking – a global chain initiated by companies such as Microsoft and entrepreneurs like Rupert Murdoch moving from production into distribution and back into production again before they can be regulated.

It is worth dwelling on this shift for a moment as it is this context which determines the significance of talking about space in the first place. As groupings cluster increasingly around bounded objectives and interest groups there has been much discussion in a postmodern time about the breakdown of metanarratives, and the loss of the typical from the landscape at the behest of multiple, fragmented identities. In a time characterized by the rampant corporate development and international capital I describe, there is a degree of brave romanticism and wishful thinking in this analysis. Some might persist in describing the social field as one of fragmentation alerting us to the proliferation of interest groups with specific claims. But again, to describe the current debates arising within ecology, race, gender and sexuality as particularistic is to misread the social history of these movements.

Particularisms can disrupt hegemonic structures, as the history of marches and direct action attests, but only and always in relation to the universals orchestrated to undermine difference and diversity. All particularities – for instance, those of new social movements such as ecology and sexuality – are constituted in the first place in a bind with discourses of universality. Culture is in this sense always a hybridity under current conditions of globalization. The peculiar effect of globalization is the syncretic emergence of connections between disparate cultures. From 1816 and the manufacture of the first telegraph in a workshop at 28 Upper Mall, Hammersmith, the moment from which information could travel faster than people, the possibility of a naive meeting between cultures diminished. The human meeting beloved of

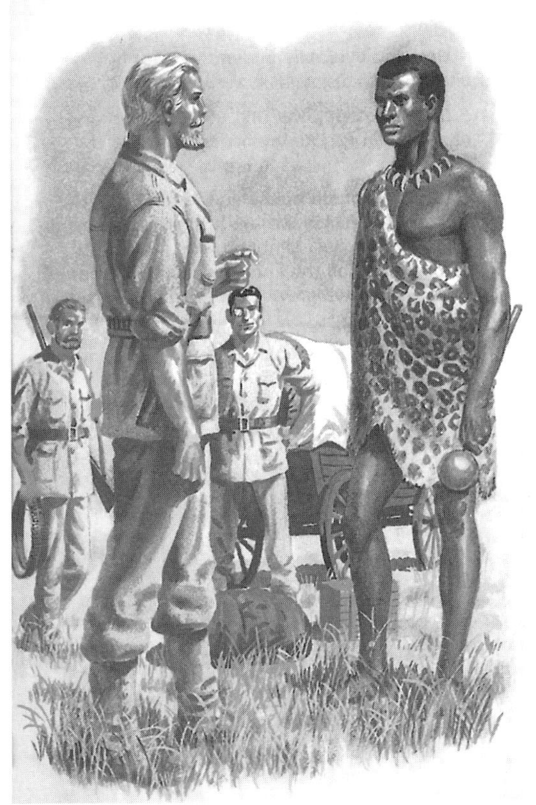

• 'We know nothing of you'. Drawing: Frank Humphris. From *King Solomon's Mines*, Rider Haggard edited by Joan Cameron. © Ladybird Books.

Ladybird books for children, with Captain Cook meeting the Aborigine, and Amerigo Vespucci the Amerindian, is now literally premeditated, premediated by the global reach of satellite and digital communications. It is within this complex layered frame that the attractions of space debate have held sway, with geographers the unsuspecting beneficiaries of a cultural mantle that passed from sociologists in the 1960s, through psychoanalysts in the 1970s, to postmodernists in the 1980s, like some semiotic blue ribband.

The publishing of late postmodernism is overflowing with geographical inquiry, while history is submerged. Space not time is the privileged domain. From postmodernism's fetishization of mapping through to the outing of the latent geographer in every unreconstructed historian, space as a social product proliferates. Where time-lords once ruled, space-cowboys now roam.

Material space has inevitably and logically given way in the popular imaginary to virtual space. But as McKenzie Walk pointed out when speaking at the 'Parallel Space' conference (Institute of Contemporary Arts, London, 5 July 1997), the virtue that lies at the root of the virtual is in question. One virtue of repetition is the possibility of learning from precedent and avoiding a farcical return of history. As virtual geographies proliferate, their spatial or architectural references appear uneasily reminiscent of the patriarchal past and do nothing yet to question the male models of insurgency into space, penetration into place and movement into territory. All the arguments of the radical geography collective of the 1970s, *Antipode*, would still seem to hold now and to do so with greater urgency. Questions of metropolis and periphery, centre and margin, north and south, still prevail with the literal meaning of antipode, the other foot, reminding us where the boot is still worn.

The current use and abuse of geographical inquiry is not surprising given how amorphous a disciplinary field geography had always been. Ripe for reinvention the catch-all inquiry that ranged from glaciers to garages found itself radicalized and refitted in postmodernism's new clothes. A century of spatial commentary was, over a twenty-year period, recovered in this makeover: Gaston Bachelard, Maurice Merleau-Ponty, Walter Benjamin, Henri Lefebvre, Michel Foucault and Michel de Certeau were restored on the shelf marked 'Space' next to their successors Jonathan Raban, John Berger, Frederic Jameson, Edward Soja, David Harvey and Doreen Massey. Of these only Massey describes herself as a geographer; otherwise space would justifiably seem to be up for grabs by everyone in much the same way as architecture makes experts of us all.

The slide towards space and away from time was not unforeseeable given what an irrelevance the Millennium has become. The impossibility of creating an adequately celebratory millennial site in Greenwich, London is surely indicative of how spurious a succession of noughts is to our deeper feelings of anxiety. Time somehow can no longer be thought at the same moment as space except in the clichéd form of the Pompidou Centre clock at the Beauborg, the Genitron, that counts down the century (even that is digital with no hands to mark the trajectory of past and future), or a millennial ferris wheel whose stubborn materiality evokes Italo Calvino's shooting galleries of the half city of Sophrania that, in his work *Invisible Cities* (1986), outstay their monumental counterparts.

The gestalt breakdown between time and space in this late twentieth century has become a rich seam for interdisciplinary practitioners whose work has always been to transform space through time to make a new history of practice. All performance reintroduces to space the duration of bodies in movement and in that meanwhile the place of performance becomes the ground for ethical relations between those bodies and the presence of an audience. Through time the ethics of performance ask not what is (now) but what ought to be (then). Performance is simultaneously futuristic and geometric, beyond itself while being beside itself. By inviting a sense of potential solidarity beyond the limits of the performance space the dynamics of time and future action flood back into the presence of the performer and audience.

• Ferris Wheel on Central Pier, Blackpool. *Robinson in Space*, directed by Patrick Keiller. Photo: BFI

Ethics in performance disturb the complacency of being. In this process the ubiquitous empty space is discovered to be brimming over with a lattice of actions and reactions, behaviours and restored behaviours, daily and extra-daily dimensions. But the discreet everyday from which performance takes its leave is the elusive other through which any shared meaning can arise. It is this everyday that spatial critique has been stalking most assiduously.

In *Theatre and Everyday Life* I joined this pursuit, aspiring to dislodge the problematic sociological category of community to a place adjacent to rather than an embracing and suffocating relationship with performance. While everyday life promised no greater conceptual clarity than community, and did nothing to limit or specify the field of inquiry any more rigorously, it did divest itself of the overtones of patronage, didacticism and care that community carried. Everyday life was also frankly more fun – within its lineage were the dislocations of the Surrealists, the idiosyncracies of Mass Observation, the psycho-geographies of the Situationists and the delinquencies and tactics of Michel de Certeau. I was, it should be acknowledged, writing this work in response to a decade of theatre practice in Europe working with projects with deep and lasting experience of specific engagement with a neighbourhood and directing a theatre workshop in south-east London which had become so embedded in the lattice of local relations as to have become indecipherable from its dynamics.

The theatre site, in Hope (Sufferance) Wharf, on the Thames downriver from Tower Bridge and upriver from the Millennium Experience, was in its day (between 1978 and 1991) a fevered intersection of performance, neighbourhood politics, contested boundaries and formative identities. The theatre was driven out by spiralling real-estate costs and overheads as riverside opportunites proliferated for developers. Between February 1991 and July 1997 that space had remained empty and derelict.

The specificity of the location of the theatre coupled with the minutiae of people's lives invited an overdetermined sense of the detail swamping the interpretative, the trees for the wood. The wood it turned out was an urban landscape moving inexorably through water-centred regeneration: the docks might have been derelict but the gravitational force of the water within them escalated local property prices. Land and its appropriation in the name of development was the object of the avaricious 1980s decade, not the street. But it was the street that carried the more immediate associations of resistance. Land was an altogether more elusive domain and how to make claim to it was all the more fraught. As the octogenarians of Bermondsey knew and demonstrated, occupation of a razed play space and the denial of the bulldozers was a far more politically charged site than reclaiming the streets with all the street-party, bright-bunting overtones of East End London 'fakelore'.

Acquaintance with the street, nevertheless, implies a theoretical legitimacy that other discredited objectivities find hard to muster in this sceptical age. Where sociology once derived its store of belief from reference to the public and the people, while anthropology continues to charge itself on the batteries of the exotic commonplace, street-talk walks the walk.

The novelist and poet Iain Sinclair has become something of an unofficial guide to, or perhaps walking companion in, this pedestrian terrain. In works such as *Downriver* (1991) and more recently *Lights Out for the Territory* (1997) he reclaims London from the vagaries of the word 'city'. Sinclair is an agitated miniaturist whose detail accumulates to landscape, worrying out the potency of niche after niche and the poetry of each street corner. His characters, including himself, a photographer and a band of cultural cohorts and everyday lifers who appear and reappear, move across territory spelling out the letters of a secret alphabet. Sinclair readily admits that choice is not the point, to notice 'everything' is the key, and this, like his auspicious predecessors in the aimless, circuitous walk of the Situationist *derive* or Mass Observation, throws up endless minutiae for speculation. Results are of no significance; when time can be spent on the process, what Sinclair calls 'enlightened boredom' or elsewhere 'ravished inattention' ensues.

Sinclair moves the reader away from the culture of consumption towards an exercise of excursion, like the filmmaker Patrick Keiller's psychic landscaping, drifting through free association. But the recurrent metaphor is that of writing, of the park as manifesto, the serial city, broken sentences among the ruins, the city as a fiction. To say that London's docks are 'an ecstasy of transcription' implies that Sinclair simultaneously occupies a site of speculation and perspective, over and above, while slipstreaming through the lower reaches of the terrain. Perhaps this accounts for the continual shifts in his prose from the terrestrial to the stratospheric with axes simultaneously operating laterally across an A–Z of ley-lines, force-fields and runes, and vertically between vantage points in the landscape and meteorological movements – the fronts, troughs and squalls of romantic weather. Looking up from the dog, from the ultimate carnivore and his small-brained master, Sinclair looks for 'a movement in the air, an unpredictable shift in the intensity of light'.

It is epiphanies like these which release the reader from the anxiety of totality that the prose rhythms set up, a redemptive quality that does not sacrifice detail to overview. They sustain Sinclair's prose in a delicate balance between the miniature and the massive, between a spatial practice, a reading and a temporal dynamics that recommend his work to anyone whose aspiration is to hold in constructive tension these apparently sundered entities.

Empty space is as abhorrent to Sinclair's prose as a vacuum is to nature. When space is de-personalized it is dogged, when it is de-canined it is tagged, and when the graffiti are gone it is laid with lines that buzz and quiver. For once you long for Sinclair to board a plane, the ultimate incongruity, to get his duty-free and release himself from the duty down below, to rise above the minutiae and indiscriminacies to see the patterns traced by his inveterate wanderings. Perhaps the derogatory comments that

• Sign to Toyota plant, Burnaston. Derbyshire. *Robinson in Space*, directed by Patrick Keiller. Photo: BFI

Sinclair's early shadow master, Peter Ackroyd, attracted for his liberal use of Sinclair's writings on Hawksmoor in his own novel of that name are indicative of the current legitimation that goes with primary experience, the walker over the secondary synthesizer. But what if Ackroyd were now invited to treat each of Sinclair's works, would there not perhaps be benefits for some whose reading eye simply can't move at the fevered pace of Sinclair's prose?

Through a hermeneutic sleight of hand, access to the everyday has implied that a return to the real is now possible. The truth might be out there, but it's also down the road if you look closely enough. Local knowledge proliferates in direct reciprocation to the loss of metanarratives that once bound district to region to nation. These might have been illusory ties, but in their stead the heavy-duty bonds of corporate finance and international capital reassert other less sympathetic relations. And it is these grander shifts of power that the street-sweepers have missed as they passed by on the sunny side.

The degree to which street-speak can be critical would seem to be an apposite question in the late 1990s. Seeking a theoretical ground for practice, unsettled by the disciplinary corrals of sociology and anthropology, troubled by the interior logics of the psychoanalytic turn and the hermeticism of literary poetics, the promises of spatial critique are beguiling: the opportunity, for instance, to shift between private and public domains, interior and exterior landscapes, local and geopolitical contexts, demographic and situationist analyses, theoretical design and structural fantasy. But these overviews more often than not defer to the charms of the gutter when that real thing, a 'local', pipes up with that spurious speech: authentic argot.

Despite this apparent flexibility, space debate is currently ricocheting between the governing dynamics of pedestrianism and panopticism. The implication that we were all subject to surveillance, read through Michel Foucault's work of the 1960s, or wrapped with ideological apparatuses and threatened by Louis Althusser's interpolation of the 1970s, gave way by the 1980s to Michel de Certeau's celebration of unobserved delinquencies in the system. Where the shadow of Jeremy Bentham's observation tower once fell upon us all, wherever 'we' were, now the tactical sabotages at play at the foot of the panopticon escape notice for just long enough to trace out some desire paths. For the 'we' now read multiple 'me's'. Total mapping has given way to contingent cartographies validated only by their subject's itinerary. As MTV moved us from technological dependency, plugged to unplugged, Peggy Phelan (1993) nudged the question of identity and gender from the visible to the discreet, from marked to unmarked.

This retreat into the crevices of the street was a necessary corrective to the overarching ambitions of the colonial imperative: to map space as a precursor to invading and appropriating it. From Brian Friel's *Translations* (1981) to Gordana Stanisic's three-week walk to Belgrade on a 'travelator ' in the Showroom, London (1994), the shift from a dramaturgy of observation to a performance of survival parallels the same two-decade shift from a poetics of watcher to watched. The fetishization of space has through these binaries emptied the ground of the politics that were once active there – politics that might look quaintly traditional now, rooted as they were in the continuities of labour, the solidarities of community, but compelling witnesses to injustice none the less. Walter Benjamin suggested it took two to tell a story: the traveller who returned from afar and the resident tiller of the soil. But the tale-teller now is as likely to be that anxious individual in a no man's land whose uncanny sense of foreboding derives from how strange home now looks.

The fulcrum between these two modes, between the Birling family's imperious view in Priestley's *An Inspector Calls* and the solipsistic wanderings of Spalding Gray's monologues, between the beholden estrangement of Beckett's Estragon and Vladimir and the aural meanders of Graeme Miller's *Sound Observatory*, has been over fifty years the axis where the symphonic social relations within theatre space have transmuted to become a plateau of competing, cacophonic voices. This move is perhaps the equivalent of architectural eclecticism, comparative spiritualities, Freud-resistant therapies and participant-observer ethnographies that have simultaneously unsettled the narratives of the theoretical field.

This movement in turn reflects the shift Ulrich Beck has recognized in a risk society, from the aspiration to move towards something good, albeit under the eye of the beholder, to the urge simply to prevent the worst. In this world the commonality of anxiety replaces the commonality of need. Here the haunted look of the fugitive returns and supersedes the community of viewers whose aspiration was to furnish a living room, to escape to the sun. The fugitive, or now I suppose David Janssen, the actor who was that fugitive, is among us all, on the run with nowhere to go, no resolution on offer, no mercy from the schedules, no hiding place.

REFERENCES

Augé, Marc (1995) *Non-Places: Introduction to an Anthropology of Supermodernity*, London: Verso.

Calvino, Italo (1986) *Invisible Cities*, London: Picador.

Colomina, Beatriz (1995) *Privacy and Publicity: Modern Architecture as Mass Media*, Cambridge, MA: MIT Press.

Massey, Doreen (1994) *Space, Place and Gender*, Cambridge: Polity Press.

Phelan, Peggy (1993) *Unmarked*, London: Routledge.

Read, Alan (1993) *Theatre and Everyday Life: An Ethics of Performance*, London: Routledge.

Sinclair, Iain (1991) *Downriver*, London: Paladin.

Sinclair, Iain (1997) *Lights Out for the Territory*, London: Granta Books.

Virilio, Paul (1993) 'The overexposed city', *Zone* 1/2, ed. J. Crary *et al.*, New York: Urzone Inc.

Stepping into the Light

Claire MacDonald

It is in space that ideas are materialised, experience experienced. Space consequently becomes the essential element in the notion of practice.

(RoseLee Goldberg)

Space contains compressed time. That is what space is for.

(Gaston Bachelard)

These notes are the marks of a struggle to keep moving.

(Adrienne Rich)

1

In the encounter between feminism and art practice, *space* has been a distinct strategic and theoretical concept and in this issue on refuge I want to discuss the meanings of space in art and activism informed by feminism, and its relationship to changing ideas about female subjectivity. In discussing space I include related associations – specifically place, location and, for the reasons Gaston Bachelard cites, time. I say art practice because I want to discuss strategies which artists use in relation to space, and I include under feminism a continuum which embraces social projects, art and activism as well critical ideas.

There are two major historical reasons for the importance of space in relation to feminism and art – and both are implied by RoseLee Goldberg's comment that it is in space that ideas are materialized and experience is experienced. It is in actual space, where real bodies meet and act, that concepts are performed – and for Goldberg and others, it was performance in the late 1960s and 1970s that offered the fruitful possibility of materializing art and art concepts. It was in *space*, and by implication time, that art theory met art practice. RoseLee Goldberg's essay 'Space as praxis' was published in the summer 1976 issue of *Studio International*, which was devoted to space. She took as her starting-point an exhibition and publication called *A Space: A Thousand Words*, at the Royal College of Art in London, which invited artists, architects, musicians and filmmakers to contribute ideas on 'the production of space'. Taking her title from Oskar Schlemmer's concept of theatre as praxis – a three-dimensional space in which the ideas about space he investigated in painting could be experienced and played out – she argued that in terms of the preoccupations of (then) contemporary artists, space was the dimension and performance the medium where theory and practice converged. Goldberg and other art critics, Henry Sayre and Rosalind Krauss among them, noted the way in which performance expanded the notions of what art was and could be, addressed the art object as commodity and allowed the context in which a work was made and seen to become part of the work itself. The performative affected all forms of artwork, expanding the fields of sculpture and painting and allowing new cross-disciplinary forms of art in which artists worked with dancers, musicians, architects and poets, to emerge. For Goldberg and others, the perception that art ideas materialized in space and through time marked out performance as the axis along

Performance Research 2(3), pp.75-84

which experimental interdisciplinary work evolved.

Though Goldberg's is not a feminist piece, the idea that it is in space that ideas are materialized could also refer to specifically feminist art and action of the time. A performative politics of place has also been an important element of feminist praxis. The practice of feminist protest has often informed the practice of feminist artists – as much when it has been problematic as when it has been successful. For feminists, the problematics of gender have often come down to confronting issues quite literally 'on the ground', whether through art activity or social action over contested sites – women's refuges and anti-nuclear peace camps being two prominent examples from the past two decades. For feminists in the 1970s it was through social action – marches and 'Reclaim the Night' campaigns in cities, the occupation of men-only spaces such as clubs and bars and the setting-up of safe houses for women fleeing violence – that theory about women's relation to social space materialized and developed. In fact, there might be said to be a continuum between art practice and social protest which reflects the connected origins of modern art and political movements in the earlier twentieth-century avant-garde. That connection is cogently explored, for instance, by Michael Newman in an essay from 1985, where he talks about feminist art after 1970 – that is, after the first flowering of conceptualism – as the only real legacy of the kind of socially emancipatory art which early avant-gardists had imagined (Newman 1986). The effect of the performative on the art object opened up lines of enquiry that informed conceptual art, land art, performance and kinetic art, and, later, photography and installation, but it was feminism, with its open-field approach – anti-formalist, broad-based politically and with a vital activist side – which continued those lines of enquiry in an active political context.

For feminists in the early 1970s the eruption of space and context into the artwork not only implicated performance as the medium where art practices could meet, but also implicated the gendered political context in which the work was made and seen. Art which responded to space and included the viewer in the work was ideal territory for feminist experiments which brought together the experiences of social activism and art-making. The bringing of conceptual ideas into live space was an example of political as well as artistic praxis, breaking the boundaries between art and politics and bringing the politics of social protest into the process of art-making.*

* See Broude and Garrard *The Power of Feminist Art*, Moira Roth's *The Amazing Decade*; and Parker and Pollock's *Framing Feminism.*

Jo Hanson has argued (1997) that 'the shift in meaning away from the autonomous object toward the physical, social or conceptual context initiated a revolutionary understanding of site-specific art, public art, studio art, and the role of the artist. It was feminist art in the '70s that created the precedents of strategies, methodologies, theories and practices that characterise activist art' (Hanson 1997).

While feminists addressed the gallery as a space and as a system which privileged the male gaze, and materialized the tradition that a woman's place in art was to be viewed rather than to make art, feminist artists often conceptualized performance art as free space, a non-historicized present-time field of operations in which to work. Exploring that space gave rise to the understanding that, even though visual artists distanced themselves as performers from the restrictive historical structures of theatre, there could be no free space. Performance was also cross-mapped with gendered histories of looking, doing and being which had to be addressed – and which then provided fertile sources of material from which to work.

In the 1970s 'space' was a concept in the ascendant, and just as devoting an issue of *Studio International* in 1976 to discussions of space shows its significance to the art world, so the devoting of a year-long seminar to the subject by the Oxford Women's Studies Group in 1977 shows the emerging importance of feminist spatial thinking to anthropology. The book which came out of the seminar, *Women and Space: Ground Rules and Social Maps*, edited by Shirley Ardener (1981), remains pertinent to discussions of women and social space, and prescient in its understanding of space as a concept. Almost as significant as Mary Douglas's *Purity and Danger*, first published in 1966, it builds in part on her work. In her introduction to the essay collection Ardener, an anthropologist, looks at how 'social maps' are drawn up and how the rules governing physical space reflect social organization. She discusses the work of Erving Goffman in relating social to spatial structures, articulates the ways in which time and space are related and points out several critical issues – that women often do not control space but mediate access to it, that spatial boundaries reflect social ones, and are reaffirmed through rituals and that the meaning of objects is profoundly related to their place in social/spatial organization. Douglas's original work analysed the ordering of social environments through distinctions between clean and dirty. Her general proposition that dirt is never an absolute category, but is always that which is not where it should be in the social order of things, and that uncleanness is simply 'matter out of place', quickly assumed the place of a paradigm shift, and a base from which further cultural criticism developed. While *Purity and Danger* is too early to be overtly feminist in the open and self-conscious way which *Women and Space* is, its insights informed feminists across disciplines – and possibly artists as much as academics.The perception that social organization of space is not 'natural' but highly systematized and bounded and that these systems have important gender implications was followed by a wave of feminist anthropology and feminist geography which opened these ideas up to further theoretical questioning through journals like *Antipode,* which kept radical, feminist conceptions in play throughout the 1980s, and Doreen Massey's work as shown in her collected essays *Space, Place and Gender* (1994).

Doreen Massey's collection of essays brings together fifteen years of her thinking as a radical, feminist geographer. Her view – that spatial thinking has been dominated by dualist and male views of space and time – is the essential starting-point for an analysis of space which includes place and its associations and which is perpetually 'unfixed'. Space-time is a network of social relations and concepts experienced differently by those holding different positions within it. Her own work is concerned with putting forward alternative readings about space and place which seem to be appropriate to the times in which we live. She addresses how we experience space, time and place, how identity is constructed in relation to these dimensions, how we might perceive them as flexible and yet have a sense of locatedness and stability. Some of the lessons learned about social space and social protest have come from setting up illustrative and contentious confrontations at highly explosive cultural breaking-points.

One of the most significant and celebrated examples of feminist action over a contested social space comes from the early and mid-1980s. The protest against the siting of Trident missiles at Greenham Common near Newbury lasted from 1981 to 1986 and involved thousands of women who either visited or lived at the camp. It is a social event which has been subject to readings, films and memoirs and is significant for many reasons. In the early 1980s the women's movement in Britain was diversifying and changing. Greenham was sited at the cusp of change in the women's movement itself, as it ceased to be a broad-based radical movement and diversified into forms of radical direct action – with links to the ecology and land movements – and a more clearly theoretical, largely Marxist feminism situated within academia and supported by a framework of journals and publishing. There is much evidence of the trauma which the splitting of the women's movement gave rise to, and the early issues of *M/F* and *Feminist Review* as well as movement documents from the turn of the decade bear witness to the fragmenting of the feminist mainstream. Events which take place at moments of high crisis tend to throw social issues into high relief. Greenham seemed for many women to exemplify a struggle between elemental male and female forces, a struggle that was being played out on the land/ground. The fact that it also concerned an American nuclear base sited on British common land added more layers of meaning to the protest.

Greenham was a defining moment for the women's movement and for feminism, partly since it seemed to articulate in stark and essentialist terms the relationship of men and women to space: the legitimated, public world of men and the marginal world of women. In a haunting image from the mid-1980s, a group of women stand by the perimeter wire, outside the fence. They are literally on the edge, on the outside looking in. It was a protest which, towards the mid-1980s, was increasingly articulated in performative terms; women placed symbolic objects on the wire – almost like votive offerings or talismans. Their presence was extremely disturbing to the soldiers in the base and was seen in terms of a kind of elemental male/female confrontation. Caroline Blackwood, who visited the camp extensively in 1984, says of the treatment of the women by local people: 'youths from Newbury came down in the night and poured pig's blood and maggots and excrement all over them. Red-hot pokers were shoved through their polythene benders in order to terrify them' (Blackwood 1984: 8).

The compressed time of the common land they stepped on to was a space composed of dense historical connotations. The symbolic implications of the Greenham protest as a social performance are discussed by Peter Stallybrass and Allon White in *The Politics and Poetics of Transgression* (1986). The context for their reading is the symbolic nature of transgression: where the critical points of social formations are to be found, those areas which are considered to be marginal – dangerous thresholds on the edge of social stability. The locations they choose – the fairground, carnival, below-stairs in Victorian life – are parts of social life and culture which are overlooked, considered trivial or even meaningless, but, as they note, what is socially peripheral may be symbolically central. Their discussion draws on Mary Douglas and illuminates the meanings of the kinds of actions Caroline Blackwood describes – for Stallybrass and White the symbolic actions of the women themselves invoke 'mythopoetic transgression' and draw from their antagonists a similar 'material symbolism'. Greenham women were out of place, out of jurisdiction, crossing geographic and spatial boundaries that represented important social boundaries.

Greenham was always problematic, for feminists as well as for others, not for its principled and courageous stand against nuclear weapons but for its imagery. The 'mythopoetic transgression' which Stallybrass and White cite was in part the invoking of other historical radical movements based on common land – for example, the Levellers and Diggers – and in part the invoking of mythic antagonism between men and women which identified women with the earth, nature and peace, and men with technology and the rape of the land. In mythic confrontations there is no conversation space. There was, of course, also a sense of urgency which it is now hard to recover. Readings of the events underline the ways in which social maps are grounded. Greenham provides complex evidence for the analysis that Ardener, Stallybrass and White and later Doreen Massey were making. I am not arguing that Greenham could have been approached differently – apart from anything else social movements have their own momentum; at least part of the way the protest developed was organic and self-perpetuating. I am pointing to its importance as a model of how women were addressed *materially*, from within the culture, once they transgressed certain boundaries. I am then interested in looking at what kinds of strategies artists and critics have developed to address the kinds of problems raised.

2

There is a phrase from an essay of Linda Alcoff's in which she brings into play the idea of feminism as a continual process of becoming, a project in the making, always looking toward the future; she says that the feminist subject is always 'emergent from historical experience' (Alcoff 1989: 433). I like to imagine the female subject as a swimmer, perpetually breasting the waves, clearing the surface, getting her head above the sea of history. It is a phrase reminiscent in some tangential way of Gaston Bachelard's observation that space is compressed time. To step into space is to draw the history of that space around you and animate its possibilities. Alcoff's essay, written in the late 1980s, was intended to counter some of the reductive tendencies of feminist thinking which saw feminisms – radical, socialist, cultural and the rest – as separate and in standing opposition to one another, rather than as divergent strands in a creative mainstream.*

In viewing feminism as a process of becoming, always contingent and never closed, she relinked it to activity, to tactics, strategies and to making. I want to consider that idea, in which the emergent female subject remakes herself by drawing on strategies of the past and bringing history with her, and to look at the way in which the histories of feminist art and social protest are present in current artworks that have space and place as their common factor – I don't want to call them site-specific, rather to explore the ways in which they draw on material sites, conceptual sites and ideas about space and the real, troubled histories of social protests.

* This debate can be followed in many recent books and articles, I would turn the reader's attention particularly towards Judith Grant's *Fundamental Feminism* and Elspeth Probyn's *Sexing the Self.*

The British artist Rose Garrard's career spans almost exactly the period of second-wave feminist activism. Her art maps out a performative space which allows differences and conflicts to be actively aired without resolution, in which artist and viewer can collaborate to investigate meaning and can be seen as 'problem-solving'. Rather than drawing attention to issues or highlighting crisis, her work uses process and performance to work through alternative possibilities. She articulates a feminist space/time – a multidimensional space in which hierarchies of value and linear narratives are transformed into constellations of elements into which there are multiple points of entry.

In the introductory essay to Rose Garrard's 1994 exhibition catalogue *Archiving My Own History*, Louisa Buck talks about the ways in which Garrard's work 'interrogates the boundaries' of art history, saying that in 'mapping the shadowlands' she 'proposes alternative sets of co-ordinates from which to plot a new, more authentic terrain'. That 'more authentic terrain' is not a place of fixed identities. In proposing change Garrard does not want to substitute one set of values, a feminist one, for another. Garrard marks out conceptual and cultural maps on the ground, in real time and real space, creating imaginative spaces which allude to the possibility that art can liberate the social imagination and touch personal experience. In her most recent works she brings together three decades of art practice and feminist experience in a series of works she calls 'conversation pieces'. Multi-media and time-based, they use a given space as a frame within which the meaning of objects and events is animated. The public activity of making becomes a process-based performance which invites the participation of the viewer. The space in which she works literalizes the idea of praxis as a place where theory and practice meet.

Formally her work takes up the insights and practices that RoseLee Goldberg discusses in 'Space as Praxis'. The notion that the work of art was unfixed in meaning until completed by the viewer was one of the outcomes of moving the emphasis of art practice away from the complete, discrete object and towards a process and experience-centred view of art. Equally important was the extension of the frame of the work into space. The work could then include the viewer, the qualities of the space and the potential events which happened within its conceptual boundary. In Rose Garrard's first cited work, *Boundaries*, her graduating show in 1969, viewers walked amongst life-sized figures in a room of mirrors in which the floor was covered with sand. While the piece is formally simple it stages a vocabulary of strategies – the viewer is implicated as performer, almost as collaborator, and is asked to consider her/ his own position. The whole space is used and the relationship amongst the objects in the space is animated by the viewer.

• Rose Garrard, *Edge 88*, Slaughterhouse Gallery, London.

In later pieces the quality of the objects themselves and the ways in which they 'behave' in space become much richer and more textured. As well as operating in the present, Garrard starts to include references to the past, to time, memory and history – she begins to insert a feminist presence into the work so that the exploration of artistic strategies was used to explore gender issues and ideas. For her, theory has been the outcome of the art practice and in looking at the development of her work her pragmatism is very clear; she tries things out in space, on the ground, to see what ideas emerge from them. She would not call herself a performance artist, though performance is an essential part of her work – just as she would not call herself a sculptor, a video artist or a painter, though all these media form part of her work. The use of her own live presence is a repeated strategy within the work, though she does not work with performance in every work.

Her practice now spans almost thirty years, coterminous with the women's movement. Her refusal to settle the terms on which her art can be categorized can best be seen as a refusal of closure – one of the key ways in which her artistic strategies and feminist theories meet. The work refuses to be fixed in time or in place, is ephemeral and always returning to the necessity of the dialogue between viewer and work in producing meaning. The viewer has to 'act' on the work to animate its meanings, just as the artist 'acts' in and on the work to animate it.

Of the final works archived with the 25-year survey documented in *Archiving My Own History*, several have been made in response to complex political situations. In *Calgary Conversation* the artist inhabited a gallery space for each working day of three weeks, holding conversations with visitors while beginning to map out the space with objects and fragmentary drawings relating to

• Rose Garrard, *Calgary Conversation*, Calgary, Canada, 1993.

questions of colonialism in Canada. After every exchange each visitor was asked to contribute a handprint to the wall, 'as an act of continuity and mark of public action rather than agreement' (Garrard 1994: 74). The work exhibited at the end of the process, once many ideas had been brought together, represents the traces of a field of operations which attempts to recognize the unfixed nature of place and time and the different positions which subjects hold in it. In *Disclosing Dialogues* similar kinds of strategies created the work. Judith Mastai, a Canadian critic who participated, describes Garrard's process as one of animating that which remains dormant until her 'body and intelligence' initiate the making process that frames the experience of time and place. The work 'remains as a history to mark the fact that we were here, then' (Garrard 1994: 77). If the claims sound modest – conversation, exchange, lack of resolution – then perhaps they are. They need to be seen in relation to the potential conflagration emerging from confrontational social issues and the importance of this kind of contemporary art in engaging with and illuminating the way we live and see the world, linking it to conceptual ideas like Doreen Massey's, to which Rose Garrard's ideas are very close, rather than attempting to impose restrictive framing. They are works which open out towards other ways of being, doing and engaging: as if after twenty-five years of art-making the artist has learned to do less in order to do more.

It is not a paradox to suggest that Garrard has always had a very strong sense of the importance of art and artists in leading towards the exploring, deconstruction, dismantling of fixed ideas – it is much more that along with many political artists she has also sought to rethink the idea of the artist herself. What Garrard's work exhibits is the intention and success of an artist whose work originates in personal experience but does not involve retelling it, or taking on a persona. Instead the persona emerges in relation to the work, and the space in which the work takes place.

Strategies developed by feminist artists and theorists in the 1970s, combined with the experience of feminist social action up to perhaps the end of the 1980s, have made a significant contribution to the creative mainstream of art practice internationally. At the beginning of this article I talked of 'art and activism informed by feminism', rather than 'feminist art'. Feminist art enlarged our vision of what art could be – and performance often acted as a laboratory practice in which ideas about the self, the body and its spatial/temporal context could be explored. The streams of practice that characterize the interconnected, pluralist worlds of art and theory today bear witness to feminist engagement but there is no longer a simple division between feminist and other art. Instead it is possible to find feminist moments of transformation, processes and methods which draw on feminist ideas.

In contemporary work which takes space, place and location as its starting-point – and often subjectivity in relation to space, often with a performative element – it is possible to see developments of earlier feminist strategies which address some of the earlier problems of addressing social space through symbolic performance. In a parallel way, much of the new politics of place in today's Britain – for instance, the developing critique of land and space around road developments – draws a significant part of its energy from radical feminism but has refined its tactics. There has been an important process of exchange in which artists and art ideas have increasingly been part of articulating and raising consciousness about social issues. This has been particularly so amongst road protesters, where artists have taken part in political action, as at the Newbury by-pass protests, or where protesters have defined their sites in art terms, creating ritual performances and installations such as 'car-henge' at Pollockshaws in Scotland.

Most importantly though, protesters have, like artists, sought to illuminate the layered 'compressed time' of chosen sites, bringing historical moments and associations to life in ways that identify the complexity of sites rather than using them to illustrate historical, and mythic, confrontations.* This is, of course, only partly true and is not to say that bitter political protests over land do not take place in other contexts; I am writing this at the end of a complicated week-over standoff and protest in Northern Ireland, which saw a small women's peace camp swamped by protesters – but I am also reminded that in the 1996 marching season (by Loyalist Orangemen) there was a strong presence of art-based tactics for diffusing confrontation: the kind of tactics outlined in an earlier issue of *Performance Research* by Dan Baron-Cohen.†

* See, for example, Jay Griffiths's discussion of protest culture in his diary piece in the *London Review of Books*, April 1997.

† See his article, 'Resistance to liberation: decolonizing the mindful body', *Performance Research* 1(2): 60–74.

One of the lessons of Greenham Common was simply that the ways in which social maps and physical boundaries cross and coalesce fuel very real material tension, and explosions of antagonism are hard to live with. Art practice has often allowed women artists to place risky and confrontational actions in contested locations within a frame which allows them to be read and understood as art, and then assimilated more widely into social discourse. There are new strands of art practice which have continued to work across the boundaries of social protest and have refined that work to include the insights from feminist theory and practice – learned through the many events and actions which took place in locations in and outside the definitions of the art world. These art forms should not be thought of as separate spheres but rather as indicating the way in which contemporary art can no longer be seen in terms of its disciplinary practice. It can be better understood as a constellation or an interlocking series of plural spheres which artists may work with.

This work has drawn from both feminist social action and from art discourse in order to work with space and place. The origins of performance in social protest have been combined with the communitarian, anti-gallery ethos of the 1980s. When artists work with sites they begin to include within the remit of the work the location itself and to draw attention to a constellation of possible performative practices associated with space and place, which may either be seen as art or, indeed, remade as art.

Performance is often used to animate the space rather than to use the site as a framework for preconceived action. Performance might be said to be site-dependent as well as site-sensitive, it exists in order to uncover the meanings implicit in the site – you might say it operates by extending the work into space in order to bring place into being. The public sphere continually offers up contested, gendered space as a rich source of ideas and possibilities not only for artists but also for divergent ways of imagining the way we might be, might live better.

In the early spring of 1997, before the British general election, a girl called Animal emerged from a tunnel at the A30 road protest site. By quitting school and staying underground in order to protest against the building of yet another road through the countryside she won the admiration of that part of the community which saw her behaviour as part of the general opposition to the then Conservative government and its decrepit, sleazy values. Clever, articulate and filthy she was treated to media coverage which implicitly approved of her life-style and gave credit to her courage and commitment in standing up to corporate bullying. The public support and the sympathetic press would have been unthinkable fifteen years ago in the early throes of Thatcherism when the women of Greenham Common were jeered and daubed with pigs' blood by local men and refused service in the shops of Newbury. Things were different then and the sites of bitter political contest have moved on. Public feeling over the preservation of the countryside is such that a girl like Animal steps into a new kind of public space, one cleared and articulated both by previous generations of protesters, from the Aldermaston marchers to the women of Greenham, and by the artists and critics who have developed an imaginative geography of political and social space.

I was in America when Animal resurfaced. I found her press images haunting, partly because I too have a 16-year-old daughter who was very far away, partly because I identified with Animal's parents, an artist and a teacher who fully supported her choices. I liked her ungendered, self-ironic name and her choice of social action over school (for the moment). As a critic I found myself wanting to pick up the thread of her actions and trace them symbolically to other stories of the flight of daughters underground. Others have noted the ways in which the figures of Animal, Swampy and the wider protest culture have fitted into powerful social myths. As Jay Griffiths said in the *London Review of Books*, 'The national imagination was gripped by Swampy, that tuft of a man, precisely because the national imagination was brought up on images of Jack the Giant Killer' (Griffiths 1997). Road protests have become the scene of strange alliances of class and culture and stages on which all sorts of ideas about history, myth and ways we might live in the future are played out. The politics of space is ever present, always filled to the brim with historical resonance, ever contested, ever highly charged. Like Swampy, Animal invoked myths, a contingent, related set. That image of a girl emerging in the spring from dark to light after her sojourn underground exists on the margins of feminist myth. Her journey was not framed as art but it might have been, in a slightly different context. It might be something artists do, and increasingly have done over the past twenty years or so as they have tried to map social space and extend its imaginative boundaries. It certainly evoked, if fleetingly, the image of a new kind of female subject, not a theoretical one but an actual one treading the boundary of myth and experience in the cause of social change.

Animal's actuality virtually drips with myth and meaning – and theory too for good measure. She is an alive theory about the world, replete with associations of women and the underworld, from Persephone to the girl in Grimm's *Household Tales* who stepped on a loaf of bread to cross a puddle and went careering down to adventure in the world of faery. Her actions, to me, build on her feminist and activist predecessors – she doesn't have to acknowledge that, it is part of the history she brings with her as she travels.

There are now cultural manifestations which draw as a matter of course on a feminist past and its lessons, often hard-learned. Actual events which bear a multi-stream influence, not so much post-feminist as new-pluralist. A significant element is by women artists. By no means all are women, but the manifestations are studded with feminist strategies and concepts, consciously or not, because feminism was and is possibly the most connected and coherent social and artistic movement of the past three decades, so close and so big it is almost invisible – as if we have a blind spot in its presence. Feminism opened the way to new practice and it opened the way to remake the female subject in relation to her space and her time – not just for art but for the imagination. In the space of my imagination I view that female subject now. I see her doubly articulated: as one of my generation swimming purposefully, still doggedly breasting the waves of history, still just getting her head above water; or, like the graceful Animal, wearing her journey to the surface more loosely as she steps into the light.

REFERENCES

Alcoff, Linda (1989) 'Cultural feminism versus post-structuralism: the identity crisis in feminist theory', *Signs* 14(3) Spring.

Ardener, Shirley (1981) *Women and Space: Ground Rules and Social Maps*, London: Croom Helm.

Bachelard, Gaston (1969) *The Poetics of Space*, Boston, MA: Beacon Press.

Blackwood, Caroline (1984) *On the Perimeter,* London: Heinemann.

Broude, Norma and Garrard, Mary D. (eds) (1994) *The Power of Feminist Art,* New York: Harry N. Abrams.

Douglas, Mary (1970[1966]) *Purity and Danger*, Harmondsworth, Mx: Penguin.

Garrard, Rose (1994) *Archiving My Own History: Documentation of Works 1969–1994*, Manchester and London: Cornerhouse and South London Gallery.

Goldberg, RoseLee (1976) 'Space as praxis', *Studio International* (July/August).

Grant, Judith (1993) *Fundamental Feminism: Contesting the Core Concepts of Feminist Theory*, London: Routledge.

Griffiths, Jay (1997) 'Diary', *London Review of Books*, London, 8 May.

Hanson, Jo (1997) *Women Artists' News* (Spring): New York.

Massey, Doreen (1994) *Space, Place and Gender*, London: Polity Press.

Newman, Michael (1986) 'Revising modernism, representing modernism: critical discourses of visual art', in Lisa Appignanesi (ed.) *Postmodernism: ICA Documents 4*, London: ICA.

Parker, Rozsika and Pollock, Grizelda (eds) (1987) *Framing Feminism: Art and the Women's Movement 1970–1985,* London: Pandora.

Probyn, Elspeth (1993) *Sexing the Self: Gendered Positions in Cultural Studies*, London and New York: Routledge.

Rich, Adrienne (1994) 'Notes towards the politics of location', in her *Blood, Bread and Poetry: Selected Prose 1979–1985,* London: Virago.

Roth, Moira (1982) *The Amazing Decade: Women and Performance Art 1970–1980*, Los Angeles: Astro Artz.

Sayre, Henry M. (1989) *The Object of Performance*, Chicago and London: University of Chicago Press.

Stallybrass, Peter and White, Allon (1986) *The Politics and Poetics of Transgression*, Ithaca, NY: Cornell University Press.

A–Z: (R–T)

A conversation with Iain Sinclair

Alan Read

Iain Sinclair talking to Alan Read at the Mayflower pub, Rotherhithe, south-east London, and walking to Tower Bridge on the Thames Path, 10 July 1997

South

This isn't really my side of the river, south. I'm not really sure what I am doing here. When I came through the Rotherhithe tunnel I thought I had dropped into a limbo, into another territory. And in the midst of all this, the Norwegian Seamen's Mission, the Church for the Deaf, I stumbled across Prince Lee Boo's grave, a Palauan prince brought back from the Pacific Islands by a Rotherhithe mail boat.

Tunnel

The tunnel joins two completely disparate cultures, locks them together. It is like a border between life and death, between two different systems of time, both banks of the river have a different usage of time. Rotherhithe is connected up to voyages out and escape, most particularly for me through the work of the poet David Jones whose grandfather was a shipwright in Rotherhithe. In the *Anathemata* Rotherhithe and shipbuilding are woven in among the Welsh material, scraps of Latin and calligraphic imaginings, all written in Harrow on the Hill. So Rotherhithe is a fanciful non-London connecting up with the oceans of the world which the other side of the river does not have.

The docks on the other side were all about minor piracies, fiddling of cargoes, and an easy walk from where I live. To cross the river by tunnel is cheating, just like the one to France. If you do something like that you are bound to end up with fires and chaos because it just shouldn't happen. There are magical prohibitions proven by doing this. The way to cross the river is a struggle on a boat. Or a long massive excursion. Like walking to artworks, the time it takes to get to the artwork you are going to view, the way you approach it is a very important element of what you are looking at. It prepares you for the thing you are going to see. If you are going to take the artwork as a serious spiritual experience, that is.

Above

I took a helicopter trip, from Hendon via Kew and Canary Wharf, directly over my house and then back to Hendon. What you see from up above is not shocking. I imagine that aerial perspective anyway. It is a kind of shamanic perspective, with Icarus-like figures who came into London by air floating above the buildings. When you are so used to poring over the maps and the early diagrams not a lot is gained by sitting in a cocoon getting that aerial perspective because it is not of your own volition or control. There is an abdication of your own sphere of operation. It might be a gentle visionary experience – I loved drifting over suburbs, patches of grass coming into places where there are flashing lights off swimming pools. But coming into London, by night, by aeroplane, is the nearest thing to dying there could be, having

Performance Research 2(3), pp.85–90 © Routledge 1997

this whole flash of the city, its beams of light and crystalline structure. But it's not me and goes against everything I feel comfortable with. If you have walked there you are still locked to base. It's very important to me that the old tumbledown house packed with all the books and information is there as a starting-point, you go away from that and if you have walked it then it is within reach, if you have switched off and leapt into a plane then it's all burnt.

Texts

The city is like the House of Memory. The way of remembering was to picture a building, and a room would represent texts or memories. So if I picture London each district and each building then has a series of texts. Things fold back from that building.

Books

They stick to you. I feel like one of those vagrant figures in an enormously large coat with pockets ballasted with books. In a sense it keeps you warm, it is a kind of fuel. There is always something to reach into your pocket for. You may suddenly be arrested, banged up in a room or cell. It would be a total nightmare if you didn't have books in every pocket. If you did it wouldn't matter too much.

The Fugitive

It has to be American. In England you can't have road movies or anything like that genre because there is nowhere to go, the place is so small. You get in a car and within sixteen hours you are as far as you could possibly go, you are at the ultimate extremity. Whereas in America you have the Olsonian thing about journeying West, the quest is possible and the great plains in the middle are like the ocean. Sam Peckinpah can change Major Dundee into Moby Dick. It's all on a much grander scale. England is incredibly petty. As a book dealer I ran over the entire country in a number of years just diving into second-hand bookshops.

Hiding

The horror now is that we are all logged all the time and it's not two-way traffic, because although the buildings are forever photographing us as we perambulate along the street we are not allowed to pick up a camera and turn it back on to the same building. If you turn a little camera back on any of that someone will come out and challenge you. Tom Phillips has been doing a circular walk over twenty-five years. One of the things he photographed was a Gents urinal. It was active in the 1960s when he started and then it just became boarded up. As he stopped to take out his camera, men appeared and challenged him and threatened to punch him up – they were postmen sneaking off early. There are people doing jobs who don't want to be photographed or else there are snatch squads who appear with guns and flak jackets if you lift a camera. It's not a fair exchange of consciousness at all and that I feel very uncomfortable with. I don't mind them photographing me as long as I've got access to photograph them.

Surveillance

Surveillance is everywhere now. During the writing of *Lights Out For the Territory* I was endlessly doing things outside MI6. Howard Marks was sitting outside there with me, he took out this massive joint and rolled it up and smoked it doing all these loud stories about the scams he had pulled and nobody took a dickie-bird of notice. Yet I was in the middle of the river with a tiny camera and within ten seconds a police launch had pulled up alongside.

Detail

The detail comes from thirty years of endless journeys, excursions and readings. Somehow all rolled up into one roll. It is like filmmaking – if you went into an editing suite with rolls and rolls and rolls of film, then start superimposing and cutting, trying to get some line that flows through it. I am cutting and shaping material from the past to fit into whatever is the present. Thus the reason why I don't have a single strand of time but multiverses overlapping.

Space

Most of the spaces, particularly those of *Lights Out for the Territory*, develop their own models that you work around. Working with the city is in *Lights Out* in the form of a labyrinth, with formal walls. The prose was circular, describing the structure of a wall and things you would find in a labyrinth such as minotaurs, bears and bulls. That is the metaphor I work with. In the first piece in the book, which was a random long V, a V sign to the city, then it is a different kind of thing, a logging on to straight lines, a horizontal structure where everything is written down on one line of time with gashes across it as something else forced its way in. You set yourself a project and the shape emerges as you get into it. You know that the plan, such as the V, is going to be undone by other things that hit you.

Film

Patrick Keiller waits. He uses the structure of the pilgrimage, the quest and the walk. But his walks are not walks. He travels by car. They are pseudo walks. And I like that. There is much more of a programme and a thesis behind what Keiller does while his has serious irony; mine is more anarchic.

Form

In *Downriver* there is a blending of poetry and methods of my past, with journalism as well because a lot of these things were done with Patrick Wright who wrote *Journey Through Ruins*. For instance, the Silvertown Memorial, a plan for a massive folly. Much of this was going out on expeditions and while he converted to journalism I was converting to fiction. He appears in there as Fredrik Hanbury. In *Lights Out* I gave the characters their real names, it explains some of the odd things that are happening in the fictions, behind the scenes.

Lee Boo

I can see people doing novels just on that story quite easily. But I never could do that. It has to be just a page or a page and a half of a much larger story. The whole meaning of Riverside London is a whole series of these stories, Lee Boo, King Cole, all of them make London interesting and without these exotic imports the city would be inert. Yet I never want to just thoroughly research one story and write about it, or even one of those A. S. Byatt novels where a journal reveals a secondary story.

City

The whole project is understanding the city, coming to terms with it and dealing with it. That is more important than any one individual item along the way. The city has become something we pour everything into at the same time as losing individual control over any kind of centre, that seems to have gone so you have more and more individuals fighting over the scraps, photographing, logging and cataloguing, because it is so economic and can be done outside any power structure. There is a general disenfranchisement, we are not all going to be invited to produce something at the Institute of Contemporary Arts, only a handful of the most extreme or academic will be invited to talk about it.

Politics

The best for me was the worst for Thatcher, when we were completely beyond power and things were just being swept aside on all fronts, that was a great time to write about because it was so vile and yet it was so energetic. You could see darkness swirling about in the skies. I think it will be much more difficult now in a supposedly beneficial climate with all that Millennial work at Greenwich.

Millennium

My natural response is horror. I want to know more about it before I can get into it. Millennial time is nonsense, it is nothing. Anyone with a sense of time knows whether it is real or unreal it is nothing. It doesn't do a thing for me. Now Greenwich as a site, with longitude, Greenwich as a site where time was recorded, and the great view of London from Greenwich Hill which was botched by Canary Wharf is vitally important to me as well as other people, Conrad, Turner included. It is one of the great viewpoints of London. It is botched as time, instead of flowing in lines, is all eddying about, whirling about in a self-reflective movie-set atmosphere, a major corruption. We bought into it but now all the roads are unilaterally privatized with security barriers, we can't walk through the road we have paid for, it is anti-pedestrian, and seals itself off. I haven't tried any magical acts to counter this. I would say the Caitling light-house was as good as anything to bring back the ghosts of a different consciousness. It casts a cyclops character, a lighthouse with its eye poked out.

Influences

I began in *Back Garden Poems* (1970) with chunks of Rousseau's confessions in a book of poems in 1970. It starts with a quote from Rousseau about walking. 'My thoughts were calm and peaceful: they were not heavenly or ecstatic. Objects caught my eye. I observed the different landscapes I passed through, I noticed the trees, the houses and the streams, I deliberated at cross-roads. I was afraid of getting lost, but did not lose myself even once. In a word, I was no longer in the clouds. Sometimes I was where I was, sometimes already at my destination, but never did I soar off into the distance.' The first piece is a London walk and some tower blocks that were then being built in Holly Street, which have now been pulled down, and photographed by Rachel Whiteread while that was happening, and the cycles of culture go around and around, while the Victorian terraces are still there. When I started out there was de Quincey's walkings, walking to the Lake District to find the Romantic Poets, as well as the American Beat, *On The Road* experience, for instance the mountain walk that Gary Snyder and Jack Kerouac do in *Dharma Bums.* There was no thesis, walking has only recently become an academic subject, it was once a way of getting around.

History

The insisting on history is a false history. Tobacco Docks, Dickens Wharfs, playing up all that industrial stuff, a lot of it very grisly as if that justifies whatever folly you are trying to put up. It is just a commercial operation. I am very uneasy about all that even if it has now gone off the boil, I think they have all been so disastrous they are now just whacking out units, somewhere to live. I notice there are big wine warehouses everywhere. You can't buy food because no one lives here at the weekend. The Range-Rovers roll out on Fridays. As ever they were artists' studios before that. It is always the first move, the property developers follow the artists in.

House

Rachel Whiteread's House did have a magical quality but there was an element of naivety and lack of imagination for what the place was as well. When it was done the nice thing was it was going to be pulled down. The petition and everything that went with it was hysteria, the intention was always to pull it down which is what made it interesting.

Fictitious Past

The pub called the Famous Angel is a case in point, a postmodern tag thrown on. At what time do you become a 'Famous Angel'? It could be the Famous Carpenters Arms, or anywhere involved in the Kray killings would mean the 'Infamous' is what you would have then. Thus the black museums work hand in hand with the heritage industry. The black museums are the Dungeons, waxworks and horrors. The police have a black museum at Scotland Yard which is like a classic museum except everything there has been involved in some major crime. Really banal objects that could be shoved out on the street in Cheshire Street or Brick Lane are there because somebody used them to kill somebody else.

Everyday

The danger here is going back to the Mass Observation with nice middle-class Communists skulking off to Wigan sitting in the corner of a pub watching people eating, drinking and reading, taking it all down not realizing that their very consciousness looking at it alters everything. There is no way you can insert yourself into a scene without also being a part of that scene. Which is one of the crucial things about fiction. At least by writing it you are putting the narrator or yourself actually into it, you are an element. The observer is an element of the thing observed.

Engagement

I want a real engagement. It is not enough just to walk down X road writing cold-blooded observations. What is the difference between the writer observer and some bag person? Very little. The observer is deeply implicated. You give the book back, people want to talk about the book and the discourse is open.

Contraries

These are systems of contraries. If you are going to follow these dogs in their mazy journey through the city you have to, by will, look up and plot the stars which in turn affect the dogs with their beams of light. We are all wired into the opposite structure.

A–Z

The woman who wrote the *A–Z* died recently. She walked London personally logging all the streets. There was a book by Geoff Nicholson, *Bleeding London*, which came out recently, one of the characters has an *A–Z* and sets himself the project of taking the whole of London and walking every single street, and while he does so blacks each one out and cancels it in the end. He continues until he finishes up with a completely black book. I like maps as fictions, I would never use one to get from here to there but staring at them is like leafing through a book, such and such a name relates to such and such a history, a beautiful shape here and there. They are all partial in some way, special interest pleading for something or other. If there was a true and total map it would be as big as London.

Maps

Some of the maps I have seen of *The Pilgrim's Progress* look not unlike the underground map of London, the moralistic map might have the 'Slough of Despond' but it is schematically drawn in, you can see it like an *A–Z* and walk it rather than as an abstraction, to return to the Tinker walking hills and mythologizing them into his moral scheme. *The Pilgim's Progress* converts the city into a moral scheme. There was once a conical earthwork alongside the London Hospital which appears in my novel *Radon Daughters*, so in a sense it is still there.

Criticism

Some have said this is politically naive and untrustworthy, but in so doing they separate language from what it is talking about, the language is really fascinating and wonderful but what it says is really dubious. I don't see how you can ever disconnect the two, langage only ever evolves in response to what the subject is. That is a general critical trope that gives people a comfortable way to deal with the work, talking about grammar and sentence structure while saying don't worry about the subject-matter.

Politics

The politics of what you are against are easier than proposing anything. We quite blatantly went through a period when it was easy to oppose. I used the books to attack magically and bring down that power structure. This was a particularly important element in *Downriver,* by doing things that would happen if things did not change. The fabulous, fantastic bits towards the end are about pushing that whole Thatcherish thing one or two steps into the ridiculous and by imagining it, not allowing it to happen, because it had already been pre-imagined. If you can call that politics it is true of the book. Trying to work magically through language to counter banal and mundane politics, in a sub-Blakean way.

Reviews

• *Memory Arena*, Munich, 1995, SpielArt Festival, Marstall/Bayerisches Staatstheater. Photo: Dirk Bleicker

The Memory Work

Arnold Dreyblatt

As an American artist who has lived for over thirteen years in West, Central and East Europe, my projects have been realized in a variety of forms, such as contemporary opera and interactive performance, installation, and publication in book and digital media. Continuing to be based on 'found' historical source materials, I have attempted to stimulate questions of memory and the collective as well as biography and 'micro-' history. During an eight-year process of de- and re-constructing what has become an enormous body of 'found texts', my work has grown to encompass the subject of 'archiving and storage' itself, which seems to reflect on the current obsessions, particularly in Europe, with a haunting presence/absence of Memory: what we choose to forget and what we choose to remember. These questions lead us to ponder the 'how, why, and

Performance Research 2(3), pp.91–104 © Routledge 1997

where' of storage and memorializing as reflected in both literate and pre-literate cultures.

In oral societies, what one could personally and collectively remember or historicize, that which one might call a 'living memory' (Hutton 1993), could be 're-collected' only through the recounting and repetition of traditions. Events have meanings for the individual (i.e. to be remembered) only in so far as they inform the collective and confirm shared traditions and values. The vocal, musical and visual imaginations fight a continual battle against the fading-away of this shared information by acting as a living storage mechanism. An art without identifiable individual voices seeks to recount the information one requires for spiritual and physical survival. Hence the importance of selection: not all information can be selected for retention; one could speak of a collective 'forgetfulness' as well as a memory. In addition, in the circular time of oral societies, history is in a sense identical to memory and dreamworld, because any chronology of historical events is remade into non-linear narrative, which serves the requirements of a collective meaning. Memory functions to negotiate transitions from past to future and to provide a glue binding the myriad impressions upon consciousness. Yet, while a pre-literate society transmits for most part within an oral tradition, it does, however, identify 'place' with 'memory-meanings'. Especially for nomadic cultures, the mapped landscape encodes markers in memory; a kind of archive of sanctified and profane locations: i.e. a holy mountain or a place where important periodic or one-of-a-kind events took place. This memory-map is not 'printed', it is rather a fluid repository of place/mnemonic associations.

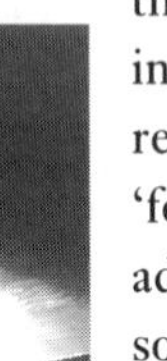

house

As we recollect, we tend to 'locate' our imaging of moments from the past in specific 'memory' places. When we reconstruct a Memory from isolated moments, separating foreground from background, our remembering takes on the illusion of space, perhaps mirroring our experience in a three-dimensional world. As Memory no longer sustains our identities, we use such terminology as 'dislocation', 'displacement' and 'dislodging' to indicate our state of alienation, and 'hidden' and 'buried' to describe the location of meaningful and often unobtainable knowledge.

With the advent of the sacred 'manuscript', the oral texts of previous eras were finally written down by privileged religious and political elites, thereby solidifying and fixing them. Since the rise of nationalism in the last century, those in power have made often irresponsible use of the remnants of this blur of collective images and origin texts in justifying the nation-state. At the same time there occurred an accelerating mania in the collection of artefacts and material records in spaces designed for access, protection and display. These 'Kabinetts', museums and archives were no longer repositories of shared values but rather of the objects supposedly representing them. 'History' accepts only the authority of 'documents' to remember and interpret the past for us. The world can be understood only through its exterior and often 'official' vestiges and traces. The collective refuge of a flexible and continually redefined 'living' memory is then replaced by sanctioned official histories, behind which lie the millions of original documents in dusty archives that are catalogued and 'put away', waiting to be 'found'.

In our current postmodern and technocratic society we are no longer in agreement about methods and structures in approaching our numerous splintered pasts. Memory exists for us not as a shared interpretation which sustains us but only in its material remnants, which either are stored externally in a passive sense or bombard us actively with information. With the transition from 'oral' to 'written' societies, oral collective memory has been replaced first by libraries and archives and now by ROM and RAM. Whereas the spatial characteristics of Memory were once collectively 'memorized' and shared but internally and individually stored, the development of the written word has externalized this process and its result. We now search in the 'physical' and 'virtual' places of library stacks, desktop folders, and unix addresses for a meaning and a history. We have lost the mnemonic techniques of pre-literate culture.

Just as our collective memories have became externalized by society, so has our individual memory become internalized as we became preoccupied with problems of personal identity and history. It is as if we have lost the mediators between the external and internal. The 'internal' memory of self and mind, explored through psychological reflections by the analytical method, mirrors but seems discontinuous from the external one. We search and scan both our 'mind-self' and the physical and virtual archives for buried meanings that may hold some sort of 'key' to connect with what has been lost to us. We attempt to fabricate a personal identity in 'historicizing' our autobiography by scanning our memories and linearizing them, much as a historian reconstructs and reinterprets events in the past. But just as the rapid piling-up of material records overwhelms the archivist and historian, so do our fractured selves have difficulty in assimilating the information overload of the postmodern age. We live only in short-term Memory, while our long-term storage capabilities seem difficult to navigate, access and process. Hence the personality which seems artificially or virtually created, in a world where, as Warhol was reported to have said, 'everyone will be famous for fifteen minutes'. There remains an irreconcilable tension between our individual experience and the images and texts which are supposed to tell us who we are.

In 1985 I found a copy of *Who's Who in Central & East Europe* (ed. Taylor, 1935) in a used bookstore (Beyoglu Kitapcilik Ltd) – near the Galanta Tower in Istanbul. The 'finding', dissection and reconstruction of this 'Memory Text' has focused and fine-tuned my attentions into an obsession over the past decade. In attempting to 'read' this work in countless meanings, renovating its sense to 'make it new', a seemingly endless array of projects and ideas has been spawned, including the Gallery installation *T: Out of the Great and Small Archive*; the publishing of *Who's Who in Central & East Europe 1933* (Dreyblatt 1995) in book form and on the Internet (1996); and performances throughout Europe of the Hypertext Opera *Who's Who in Central & East Europe 1933* as well as the site-specific interactive performance installation *Memory Arena*. For me this book is a 'found artefact' and I have treated it as a canonic and authoritative text: a 'given' or 'closed' text to which no commentary or interpretation may be added. As I first began randomly to turn the pages of this book, I found myself entering a complex network of personal and collective myth construction: a geopolitical memory of Central and Eastern Europe put together as if a puzzle were made from thousands of individual fragmentary stories, revealing an image of a vanished world captured at a critical point in time, which only a few years later would all but cease to exist. Beginning in 1990 with the commission to create the Hypertext Opera of *Who's Who in Central & East Europe 1933*, I have now spent years creating multiple pathways through this otherwise undecipherable text, resulting in thousands of pages in which the original text material had been filtered, reorganized and deconstructed in a 'cut-up' archive of collective memory. In the course of this process, while attempting to realize a hypertext in two dimensions for the book publication by Janus Press, for the Internet and in later projects, I realized that no objective, comprehensive cross-section would be possible, and that finally only portions of text would survive, in endless formats and variations. As a metaphor for this reorganization, I imagined a grid network in which verticality represents individual lifelines from birth to death (although in fact no one in this book dies, since at the moment of death one exits a *Who's Who*), while horizontality indicates the points and moments of commonalty and relationship between individuals. One might travel through one personal lifeline and then 'shift gears' laterally in a kind of virtual meeting of the 765 chosen personalities. I attempted to present a process of reading as a continual sifting and sorting

empty

through of this endless data-bank, linking fragments of information by optical and thematic association which results in a 'Biography of Everybody'. As Gertrude Stein has written, 'There will then be a history of every one who ever is or was or will be living, mostly every history will be a long one, some will have a very little one, slowly it comes out of each one' (Stein 1966).

I was also greatly inspired here by the printed and pedagogical structure of the Talmud in Jewish tradition. Here one finds multiple 'peeled onionskin' layers of often conflicting commentary and interpretation in an endless ongoing international conversation between the printed work and its living reading (which takes place out loud). It is a confrontation between a written and an oral tradition. One has the sense of entering a cross-referenced information network of ever-increasing complexity, in which all individual elements connect to each other in a kind of medieval 'hypertext'.

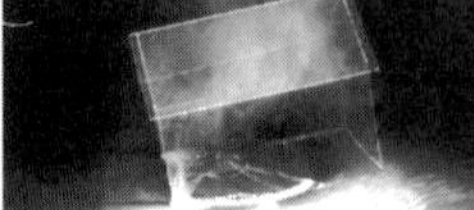

window

The years of manually sifting through these 'mountains of data' in preparing the various projects gradually resulted in an interest in presenting the living environment in which data is stored, archived and brought to life within a form which would involve the public. During a period spent researching at the British Public Record Office in London in early 1993 for a forthcoming project, I was struck by the meeting of 'high-tech' with antiquated mounds of decaying paper file folders. Through a complicated bureaucratic system of monitors, runners, helpers and guards, digitally ordered files (often on parchment) were 'dug up' in an unseen underground chamber, and then gradually transmitted by a human conveyor belt to the reader above, whose clip-on remote beeper notified him that the file had arrived.

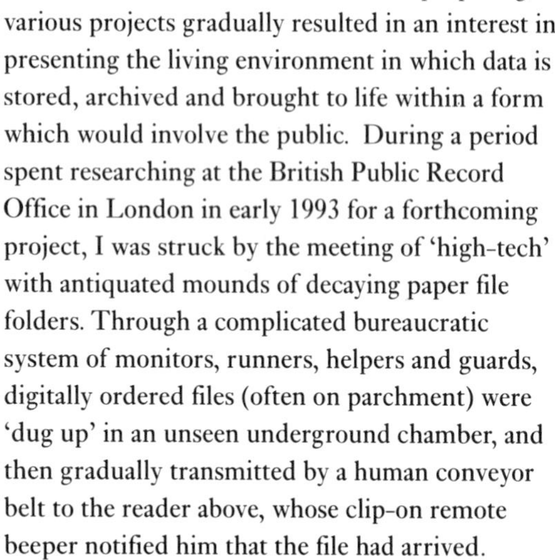

I began developing a concept for what has become 'The Memory Project' in 1991. 'Memory Arena', the previous phase of this project (a collaboration with Fred Pommerehn), was realized in February 1995 at Kampnagel Fabrik in Hamburg. This was followed by performances in October 1995 at Marstall/Bayerisches Staatstheater as part of the SpielArt Festival in Munich and in 1996 at the Arken Museum of Modern Art as part of Copenhagen '96 – Cultural Capital of Europe. In 'Memory Arena', over 700 readers participate in multiple simultaneous readings from individual files created out of the chosen 765 biographies from *Who's Who in Central & East Europe* within a very precise temporal and visual environment. A 'Reader Acquisition Team' which has been established within the city during the preparation process invites and registers individuals from professional institutions, political organizations, the arts and sciences, the media and from subcultures and minority groups, etc.

'The Memory Project' becomes in reality a functioning albeit temporary institution. It can be considered as a 'sample' of a ritual event, which may be periodic (as in once a month or once a year) or which may exist within an indefinite time-frame.

• ***Memory Arena*, Hamburg, 1995, Kampnagel Fabrik. Photo: Dirk Bleicker**

The sampled excerpt, which we know as a 'performance', is experienced either in its originally conceived form of one twelve-hour day (proposed for the 'Remise' in Vienna but never realized), in variations of three or four days, or as a long-term installation. As one enters, it seems that the event has begun long ago and that when one leaves it will continue for days or years. It acts as a sign pointing to other possibilities, thereby indicating how a participant might 'read' it in time as well as in its utilitarian functions.

'Memory Arena', has included three spaces: an Administration Area, the Arena, and the Café. Upon entering the installation in the Administration Hall, crowds are first processed by almost a hundred staff members in coloured uniforms through a labyrinth-like transit station, passing through numerous passageways, waiting and administrative areas and thematically related exhibitions. The administrative staff co-ordinate the event among the several hundred readers, the public and the hierarchical staff of archivists and bureaucrats, making sure that each individual and all written information are at the correct place at the right time and that an 'Events Protocol' is followed to the minute. The previously invited readers are processed separately from the arriving audience members. The focal point of the Administration Hall is a fully operational 'Great Archive' from which 'files' are checked out and transported to be read aloud in a central space, the 'Arena'. One of my concerns has been to simulate the process of searching, sorting and finding/accessing information, whether in the form of archive documents or digital readouts. From the beginning, this work has sought to create a forum in which the general public and guest members are invited to participate in a mode of non-linear associational reading and voicing, reflecting my methods in searching my 'Who's Who' database or in turning the pages of the original lexicon in creating my own canonic text.

In the 'Arena' itself an amphitheatre-like platform containing twelve reading stations covering three sides of the space

open

• *Memory Arena*, Copenhagen, 1996, Arken Museum of Modern Art. Photo: Jan Rüsz

surrounds the public who are able to choose between experiencing the 'collective space' of simultaneous readings from *Who's Who in Central & East Europe 1933* or moving in closer to observe the 'individual' reawakening of specific texts, creating their own 'stories' and 'interpretations'. The texts are simultaneously projected on the Memory Arena Data Wall where they are read. Computer navigations through the database are displayed throughout the entire installation complex.

The fragments of individual memory remnants which are physically located in archival storage are 'brought out into the open' within a vocalized collective forum. One reflects on the fragmented subject, since the hypertext collage refers to persons who no longer exist (however, there are no death dates in a *Who's Who*: when a person dies he or she is no longer eligible) we are left with a sampling of biographical shards. The participants often request additional biographical or background information, or scan for a narrative or ideology. We realize that a few lines sent in to the publisher in Zurich in 1933 is all which remains, that the subject of the piece serves only to pose questions about identity and history, rather than to answer them. Gradually one comes to cherish a few scaps of meaning, a birth date, a book title, a pregnant phrase; only to ponder later the document which will contain what little evidence of own's existence will remain in fifty years.

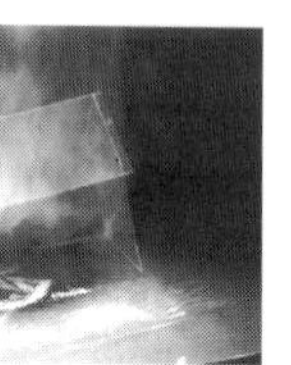
door

There therefore results a continual exchange of roles between performer/participant and visitor/public. Members of the general audience who wish to take part as readers may apply at the appropriate desk in the bureaucracy and are then integrated into the system. At any given time in the arena, well-known local or national personalities might be found simultaneously reading next to 'unknown' persons, all of whose professions are displayed prominently on their name cards and on the Data Wall as well as on the 'Protocol' blackboard in the Café area. A relativization of public and private image therefore takes place. At all times one finds oneself observing the movement and behaviour of others passing through the institution, at the same time being aware that one is likewise a 'player' for the others just by 'being there'. While interactivity in performance or installation is usually realized within a simplistic cause-and-effect situation, the Memory Arena enables one to connect and understand through complementary levels of participation. One may utilize the holdings of the Archive or the Computer Navigation Centre for further research in paper or digital form; one may wander in the exhibition display areas or take part in a social situation within a mix of 'performers' and 'public' in the context of a 'café area'. Sound installations and data displays transfer the ongoing ritual in the Arena to other areas. It is through a kind of 'wandering' and 'passing through' that one is given an opportunity to establish one's own meanings in an active sense. We find ourselves posing a single question: 'How will the past be remembered as it passes from living memory into History?' (Hutton 1993).

REFERENCES

Dreyblatt, Arnold (1995) *Who's Who in Central & East Europe 1933, Eine Reise in den Text,* Berlin: Janus Press; on-line: http://www.uni.lueneburg.de/memory/ (in collaboration with the Kulturinformatik Department of the University of Lüneburg, Germany.

Hutton, Patrick H. (1993) *History as an Art of Memory*, Hannover, NH: University Press of New England.

Stein, Gertrude (1966[1925]) *The Making of Americans*, New York: Something Else Press.

Taylor, Stephen (ed.) (1935) *Who's Who in Central & East Europe*, Zurich: Central European Times Publishing.

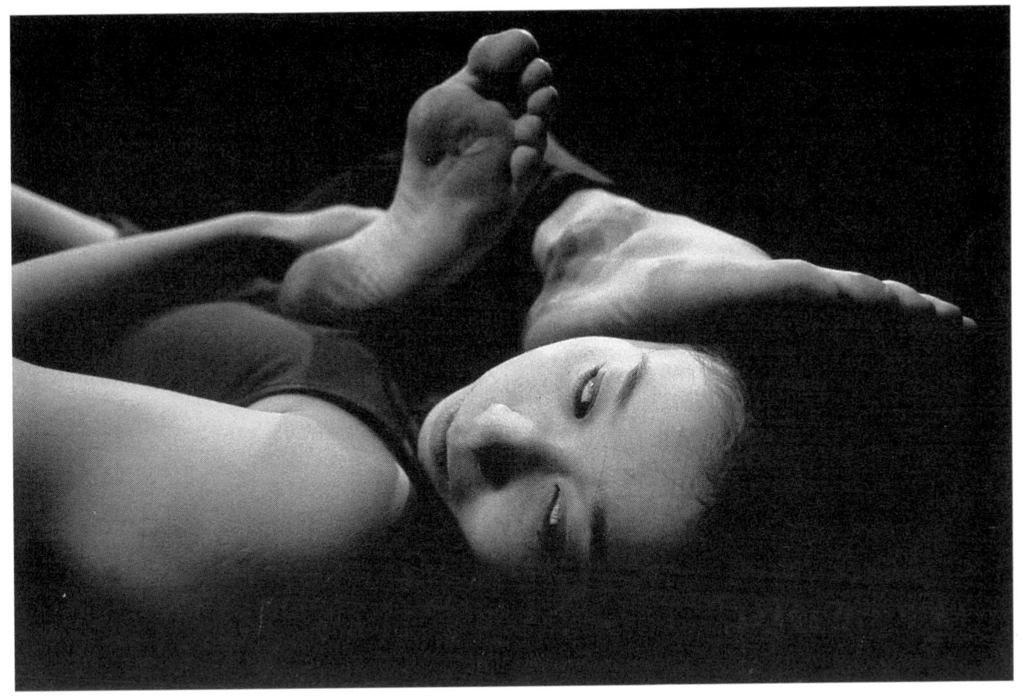

• *Splayed Mind Out*, Gary Hill and Meg Stuart. Meg Stuart/Damaged Goods, 1997. Photo: Maria Anguera de Sojo

Cultural Unconsciousness in Meg Stuart's Allegorical Performances

Rudi Laermans

ONE

In 'Against Interpretation', probably one of her most influential essays, Susan Sontag advocates the necessity of a new attitude within the realm of the arts: we have to learn (once) again the practice of 'just looking'. We usually contemplate pictures or performances in view of understanding; we observe works of art as meaningful communications, we 'read' and treat them as texts; we try to grasp a message or a coherent series of interrelated meanings. This sort of looking does not enjoy itself without the intellectual capacity of 'looking through', the skill or competence 'to see more' than one can see at first sight. The act of looking is thereby assigned a supplement, and this addendum – i.e. the will to understand – rapidly becomes the essence of looking itself. Contra this dominant aesthetic attitude, Sontag speaks out for 'an erotics of art' against a 'hermeneutics of art'.

Sontag's passionate critique of an interpretive stance towards works of art was obviously inspired by her admiration of the work of, amongst others, John Cage and Merce Cunningham. In 'Against Interpretation', Sontag indeed tried to legitimate the second, postwar (after-)life of modernism in the United States. The edge was taken off the well-known argument of incomprehensibility, so often put forward against the art of Cunningham or

Cage, with the quite simple but effective thesis that the attempt to comprehend the artwork as such was wrong. 'Just watch or listen': thus sounded Sontag's message against all those who complained of the absence of any clear meaning in modernist art.

About the same time – the mid-1960s – that modernism became the new official canon, a completely different sensibility broke through in the circles of New York-based artists. This new sensibility was the subject of another famous essay by Sontag; during the next decades, the vague label 'postmodernism' gathered a steadily increasing following amongst scholars and critics when reference was made to pop art or movement research – but this is not my subject here. The most striking feature of the images of filmmaker John Mekas, of Andy Warhol's multiples, or of the performances of the Judson Church group (Steve Paxton, Trisha Brown, Carolee Schneeman ...) undoubtedly was the pairing of formal radicality with expressiveness. The chosen stylistic means, such as mass cultural icons (Warhol), or pedestrian movements (Judson Church), did not signal a total break with modernism's essentialism. On the contrary, they rather enlarged the vocabulary of modernism – of, for example, 'pure' images, or 'pure' movements. Not that the arts again became 'talkative'. Warhol's pop art or Judson Church's movement research was communicative, but in a highly ambiguous way; something was said, but the message contained no univocal information. 'The medium was the message' as Marshall McLuhan had put it, and the resulting communication was 'something like 'communication . . . without communication' (J. F. Lyotard). This was neither empty formalism nor naive expressionism.

broken

Actually, the new generation of artists explored aesthetic forms characterized by the polysemy of allegory. The latter expression is used here less in a literal way, and rather in the primarily connotative mode of Walter Benjamin's writings. Thus, allegorical art has to do with the making of '*Denkbilder*', of 'thought-images' or 'conceptual pictures'. It offers images that condense one or more thoughts in a figurative, not necessarily metaphorical way – without an accompanying caption, without a clear communicative intention, without paraphrase.

I recall this history – excellently documented in Sally Bane's *Greenwich Village 1963* – because of its importance for the work of Meg Stuart. From her first performance onwards (*Disfigure Study*, 1991), this young, Brussels-based American choreographer has quite explicitly conversed with 'the historical moment of Judson Church'. She indeed tries to recapture the moment of radical movement research within dance history, the moment of a freestyle improvisation not guided by an idea of 'dance'. Thus, in October 1996, Stuart organized the *Crash-Landing Project* in the studio at Klapstuk (Leuven). This series of collective improvisations between 'movers', musicians, DJs and visual artists, will be repeated this year in Vienna and Paris. But also Stuart's own work is obviously based on the art of movement improvisation. Through a keen combination of music, lighting, props and costumes on the one hand, and a balanced association of often surprising movements on the other hand, her performances again and again acquire a specific freshness – as if the first time of an improvised movement has really been fixed or caught ('photographed') and can therefore be repeated over and over again. The extraordinary character of Stuart's work has indeed everything to do with the fundamental paradox of all performing art: an event – the occurrence during the rehearsal process of an unexpected movement, or of a series of surprising movements – must be made repeatable. The point of Stuart's performances is exactly that the event-quality of a non-repeatable experiment or movement improvisation can be saved only in and through the contrast with a strict frame, a well-defined set of rules.

At the same time, Stuart's work regenerates 'the moment of allegory' within dance history. Stuart clearly is not interested at all in the classical body of ballet. More generally, she does not show technical tours-de-force, bodily tricks, or spectacular images. The spectator is rather reminded of banal gestures and daily movements, or of the tics and jerks of an anonymous body: spastic-like twists of arms and legs, contorted fingers and twisted postures, crawling bodies. This is body art beyond the difference between beauty and ugliness. In a way that is very close to the impulse behind the early work of Judson Church, Meg Stuart explores the banal body, the body as energetic machine – 'the body without organs' (Artaud/Deleuze). This body constantly vibrates and pulsates; its 'signs' are fiddling hands, shoving feet, automatically repeated movements of head and limbos. In marked contradistinction with the mainstream of so-called performance art, Stuart does not just show the effects – or rather, the effectivity – of the energetic 'body without organs'. As said, the movement material is arranged, edited, 'cultivated'. This results in 'body/ bodily images' – in images in which the body again and again becomes an allegory of itself, of its singular vitality as well as of its characteristic fragility.

TWO

In the beginning was not the Word but the Image; and the Image became Flesh – or so the openings of Meg Stuart's performances suggest. For they always start with a scene of one or more human bodies transformed into an Image. These 'body/ bodily images' immediately catch the gaze of the spectator: they surprise, in the very same way as a raid or an assault. The illuminated movement of legs and feet in the beginning of *Disfigure Study*, or the twirling head that opened *No Loner Ready Made*, directly took root, and made a lasting impression on the spectator. The real force of these images is not that so much is revealed in their long-lasting after-effects, but rather the fact that even within reminiscence they refuse to divulge their secrets. Apparently, these images are so much 'image' that they never transform into words. Perhaps they are in every respect essential images: images that do not affect because of their 'meaning' or content, but by their 'being-an-image' – their 'imageness' – their particular existential quality as a specific mode of representation. In a manner of speaking, they condense these aspects of the image that make the represented ineffable because of its 'imaginary' qualities: 'the said' is synonymous with 'the way of saying', 'the message' with 'the medium', 'the seen' with the fact that one has just seen an appearance.

The opening scene of *Splayed Mind Out*, made in collaboration with the American visual and video artist Gary Hill, announced as *Insert Skin Number 3*, and presented as 'work in progress' at the end of April 1997 in the studios of Kaaitheater, Brussels: three wrapped-up bodies, a stroboscope projecting flickering light, on the rear wall – the first movements are made by light, not bodies. It takes quite some time before hands, feet, legs and arms start to move. Slowly the bodies split up; together with a fourth dancer, they subsequently move forward on the stage floor, sometimes simultaneously, most of the time in solitude. The entire sequence makes one think of a sculpture brought into being. Thus, the opening scene points to a possible connection between dance and visual art: choreography as the art of freezing bodies, of transforming the human corpus into a near movement. Such a living simulacrum of a sculpture must then be modelled, so that it discovers itself anew as a bodily form. Looked at in this way, choreography is not synonymous with giving bodies rhythm. Rather, this directing activity is a particular kind of plastic art: it deals with living bodies as if they are lifeless material. The choreography has to breathe life into this material, to animate it in the literal meaning of the word: no movement(s) without an minimum of *anima*.

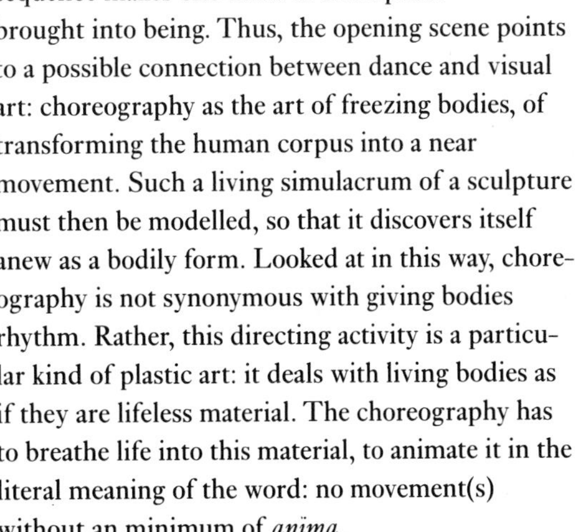

narrative

Another striking feature of the strong openings of Stuart's performances has to do with the combination of obviousness and improbability. The first sequence of *Splayed Mind Out* also has this paradoxical quality: you immediately recognize the image as possible (it reactivates a memory), and yet, the contemplation of three tangled bodies is marked by a feeling of strangeness. This oscillation between *déjà vu* and *jamais vu* is a more general feature of the 'body language' that characterizes Stuart's work. Again and again, the spectator is confronted with strange but non-surreal images: no easy juxtapositions of contrasts, no traces of striving for rhetorical effects. The presented 'body/bodily images' are always very precise and well thought out: these are indeed conceptual images, 'thought images'. Not that they represent an idea or a belief. But their particular quality seems unthinkable without the attribution to their author of an alleged 'thinking in images' or, rather, of something like 'image thinking'. In order to grasp the seen images, we must assign Meg Stuart the capability to think through images to the point where they surprise again and become unfamiliar, and also – grim.

slow

Meg Stuart's plastic language indeed balances on the tight border that separates the familiar from the frightful. Therefore, one can name her images *unheimlich* (Freud): they inhabit the realm of the uncanny. It is true that Stuart's body art makes the spectator feel uneasy. This is not an art that makes one feel 'at home'. On the contrary, the contemplated images again and again question one's basic conceptions of a healthy body – of one's own body. For this reason, Stuart's aesthetics may be called an affective one. The images she builds up in her performances are neither beautiful nor ugly, but first and foremost charged and tense. They affect, even hurt the gaze: they are 'percepts', 'blocks of affects' (Deleuze). Thus, the spectator can never really contemplate the scenes from a safe distance. Via images that simultaneously reassure and bewilder, she or he constantly becomes involved in the performance.

THREE

In a probably unnoticed way, I changed Meg Stuart into a visual artist. For the description of her work in terms of 'body/bodily images', creates the impression that after all she is more a producer of images than 'an authentic choreographer' – so that the co-operation with a downright visual artist such as Gary Hill seems obvious. But is this not too easy a thesis? Do we critics not subscribe too rapidly to highly problematic distinctions, such as the difference between Word and Image, or the opposition Body versus Voice? When confronted with hybrid performances, criticism falls back on established categories in order to offer the astonished public a clear view, an interpretive guideline. In this sense, Sontag certainly had a point in 'Against interpretation'!

It is thus no coincidence that the work of, for example, Jan Fabre or Jan Lauwers (Needcompany), both also visual artists, or of Meg Stuart, is regarded, by Flemish and Dutch critics alike, as a primary visual form of performing art. The most salient feature of these characterizations, at least as far as I know them, is their tacit silence about the particularity of an image and, related to this, the neglect of the question how a series of movements can be transformed at all into an image or a *tableau vivant*. Without comment, it is taken for granted that the reader always already knows what an image is, or consists of. Thus, a specific doxa or ideology of the Image is endlessly reproduced.

We cannot avoid questioning if the word 'image' does not point to a general mode of representation that marks out the limits of language and discourse. Is not the notion of the image – and the same question may be raised concerning the notion of sound – *qua* notion an *impossible* one, at least when considered from the point of view of knowledge (for example, semiotics or discourse theory)? Perhaps an image is exactly that which withdraws from an unambiguous linguistic representation within the visual field (or, more generally, within the textual field). An image cannot be reduced to the metaphorical addition of a number of qualified poses, movements, or gestures. An image always keeps these elements together, and synthesizes them into a particular . . . image. This transformation of an unmarked visual field into a marked image, has everything to do with the possible relationships between these elements and the emerging impressions – with the structuring and totalizing of the actual number of possibilities, or, in the language of contemporary systems theory, with the reduction of visual complexity. But a 'strong image' paradoxically conceals this constitutive act it actually is. As such, a convincing image is the unseen within the seen, the blind spot of our gaze; it falls in between the folds of our looking. Within the visual field, an image is precisely an image because all elements appear to occupy a necessary place, as if obeying an ineffable rule, an unspeakable and at the same time obvious visual melody that fixes, and fascinates, the spectator's gaze (you do *see* it, no?!). This *regard-fixe* effect goes hand in hand with the feeling that the image answers our gaze: every ('convincing') image looks back. Or as the title of an interesting study of the French art historian Georges Didi-Huberman states: '*Ce que nous voyons, ce qui nous regarde*' – what we see, does look back, and therefore concerns us: the image *affects* the gaze.

Once again: is Meg Stuart a visual artist disguised as a choreographer? Yes, she is, provided we recognise the non-sensicality of the movement language she employs in her work. Her 'body/bodily images' do speak, but in a language that induces the use of a metaphorical discourse founded upon an insoluble paradox: the word 'image' is always already a metaphor for the wordless.

But let us move on to another scene from *Splayed Mind Out* ('work in progress'): a man – Gary Hill – takes a place on a chair in front of the stage; subsequently, he starts to read from a book, an English text, in an articulated way. The interpunction is irregular, even abnormal; reading silences come at the wrong moments – the reading is one big mistake, or perhaps it is not? Anyhow, speech destroys itself: speaking is no longer a communicative act but only the physical activity of uttering words. A girl comes on and kneels; her back is captured by a video camera, and shown enlarged on a screen at the rear of the stage. She takes a pencil, and begins to write, with difficulty, with her left arm, linguistic signs – letters, combined into words – on her back. Thanks to the video camera and the screen, the public can read the words. Then the girl leaves; another female dancer comes on, improvises, and walks toward the video screen. Standing before the screen, she hesitates for a moment; the next moment, she puts one step forward and seems to disappear into the picture screen, as if swallowed up by the vanishing point – as if disappearing in that zero point holding together all public gazes. As if making visible the blind spot of our spectatorship: 'the working image' not seen when contemplating an image.

The entire scene can be easily interpreted in terms of the well-known distinction between reading aloud and writing. Yet, the scene is also very peculiar: the speaking differs from 'real speech', and a back is used as a piece of paper only in arty films (I refer, of course, to Peter Greenaway's *The Pillow Book*). The uncanny character of both acts is clearly an effect of their bodily status: speaking and writing are transformed into pure physical activities. This is obvious for the 'back-writing'. But Hill's abnormal reading style also stresses a corporality that is not usually seen at all. In the discussed scene, speaking is primarily a bodily act: Hill breathes and puffs, he audibly uses vocal chords and lungs. Thus, the staged 'body/bodily images' frame a corporality that is mostly unnoticed during communication. The spectator suddenly realizes that writing (also when done on a computer) and speaking are always physical acts. And as far as both are prime examples of meaning production, even of (wo)man's dealing with collective meaning systems (with language), the seen images show the corporal base of the predominantly idealistically Empire of Meaning. Words indeed become Flesh again.

shots

Meg Stuart's performances always fix the public's attention on the physical infrastructure – the bodily hardware – of individual and social life. Paradoxically, she succeeds in doing so by a literally imaginary contextualization of the dancers' bodies: their bodies constantly dissolve into 'strong images'. This is exactly the reason why the end of the scene just described is that striking: for a moment, a body seems to melt completely into an image. But the video is an unreliable liar, and in the next scene the dancer is again a human being of flesh and blood.

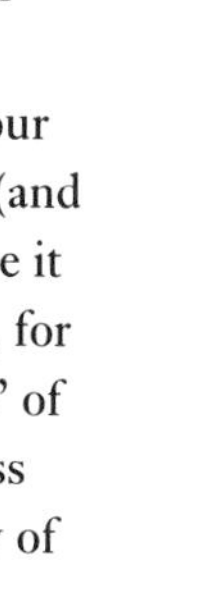

It seems to me that our banal corporality *is* our cultural unconsciousness, the unseen chimera (and phantasm!) that is always with us. But we notice it only when it starts to make some noise – when, for example, we are hungry or ill. This 'repression' of the body is the outcome of the civilizing process described by Norbert Elias in his famous study of the same name. Avant-garde art has always developed a critical stance towards this socio-cultural tendency. And so does Meg Stuart in her performances. Her 'body/bodily images' stage this cultural unconsciousness, which makes us feel uneasy. They are literally food for thought, for they direct our gaze to something that is unthought-of in daily life – to the dreadful banality of moving hands and legs, moving vocal chords, moving fingers . . . . Perhaps this ordinary vitality is conceivable only in an 'imaginary' way: by means of 'thought-images', via allegory.

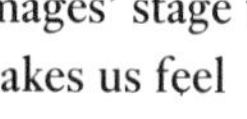

REFERENCES

Banes, Sally (1993) *Greenwich Village 1963*, Durham NC: Duke University Press.

Deleuze, Gilles and Guattari, Félix (1988) *A Thousand Plateaus: Capitalism and Schizophrenia*, London: Athlone.

Elias, Norbert (1994) *The Civilising Process*, Oxford: Blackwell.

Sontag, Susan (1994) *Against Interpretation*, London: Vintage.

back

On Emigré

Kevin Mount

Emigré is published quarterly by
Emigré Inc., 4475 D Street, Sacramento, CA 95819, USA
Publisher/designer Rudy Vanderlans
Emigré Fonts Zuzana Licko
Issue 42, 1997
80 pp., ISSN 1045-3717
http://www.emigre.com/

I carry through life the memory of having worked in a terrible newspaper office, whose beams and boards sagged and groaned under the weight of metal from which the text was pressed each week. The body type for the newspaper was made letter by letter on a Monotype machine, meaning that Enid (whose brother had been Siegfried Sassoon's chauffeur) re-keyed all the copy into a machine that converted it into punched paper tape, and that Eric next fed the tape, last-word-first, into a foundry which cast molten lead, antimony and tin into individual letter forms, packed them into syllables and discharged them in a continuous volcanic column. Then it was a matter of 1) bolting the columns of type into a frame, 2) winching them downstairs to a press, 3) belting them with inked rollers, 4) the next day smashing the whole thing into its smallest parts, 5) lugging the dismantled type back upstairs to the foundry in buckets and 6) returning all the type to the furnace to be purified. So, say 'Literature' to me and I see dead weight: I see men heaving stories about other people's lives round an ancient rotting building on metal trays; I see wedges, hammers, tweezers, mallets, bolts and keys.

Away from my lost world, the industry was long into the swing of photo-typesetting and in some newspaper offices page make-up was already being done by computer. Nevertheless I saw what I saw; I heard what I heard. Text was tonnage: it issued from an infernal region; it clanked and roared. Even the pop stars – Barthes, Wittgenstein, McLuhan – the semiologists, the sociolinguists, the semanticists, all of them wrote in gun metal. Their whispers were borne into the world on the shoulders of scornful labouring men and brought down on to a compositor's slab with a curse. 'Here's another load of shit, Vern!', 'Encore de merde, Philippe!', etc.

The revolution of the mid-1980s when desktop publishing technology began to percolate the culture, when the Macintosh computer went on sale, is inclined to be spoken of as a change of scale and volume – 'Instead of this swarming labyrinth, I give you this a little grey box with an interior fan' – when the more eloquent comparison concerns weight: 'Instead of this Titanic mass, this enormous gravity, instead of this sea-bed of memory, I bring you this mist, this veil of wishes.'

Emigré magazine started life in Berkeley, California at around the same time as the Macintosh computer. Its founding editor Rudy Vanderlans studied photography at the University of California after graphic design at the Dutch Royal Academy of Fine Arts in The Hague, home of much that was admirable about modernist European print in which form followed function. Rudy must have fancied himself the *émigré* in California: liberated, floating, stateless. 'The true émigré seeks adventuresome, romantic and human experiences', he wrote to potential advertisers in 1984. 'Their lives convey the feelings shared by the artist in us all, the feelings of boundaries ignored and the pursuit of dreams.' Emigrés that *Emigré* drew to itself included Byron, Rimbaud, Gertrude Stein, Ezra Pound, George Sand, Vladimir Nabokov. It is difficult to imagine how a West Coast design mag. born into an era of weightlessness to the music of such a mission statement, clutching a sixth form reading-list, could have lasted for more than a month, still less gained an international reputation. Except that in 1983 Rudy had met Zuzana Licko. (Pray God Zuzana Licko never reads this, since it is really nothing better than a disgraceful fantasy about the eroticism of a signature – the nought and two zeds of it!)

Zuzana was an émigré too; her family had come to California from Czechoslovakia; she studied architecture unhappily at Berkeley and there became interested in computer programming. Zuzana must have been among the very first to try designing typefaces digitally on the early Macintosh. For two years *Emigré* was produced using typewriter type, but thereafter magazine and desktop technology moved in tandem. To subsidize their work Rudy sometimes designed pages for the Macintosh trade press; Zuzana worked freelance in the later 1980s in Silicon Valley for Adobe Systems. So the central metaphor in this little story is type. Zuzana designed the fonts on which *Emigré* began to build its reputation. *Emigré* sold the fonts and supervised the discourse on modern typography – that which had been the unit of cultural weight but become the index of weightlessness. Type was once cut, engraved, punched, cast by nerveless men named Baskerville, Plantin, Kaufmann, Franklin, Cooper-Black – hear their boot-heels crunching on the gravel. Now pages are made digitally, perhaps in the 1996 typeface 'Mrs Eaves', so called after the amorous housekeeper of John Baskerville, designed and so named by Zuzana Licko . . .

lit

Emigré's great accomplishment has been to stay on the wavy edge for so long. As the graphic design theory of Rudy's Dutch school started to melt and with it the profession it engendered, so his *Emigré* hooked itself into the postmodernist design debate – where the writer may be presented as designer, the designer as writer, or both as auteur (merde!). It glamorized the academic footnote to cope with an epidemic of postgraduate research and merrily loaded its essay pages with references to Hélène Cixous, Julia Kristeva, Eco, Derrida. It poked fun at the discourse analyst's obsession with line-numbered text. It published florid prose by designers and fancy page-designs by writers, and, most engagingly, simultaneously – as an antidote to its own pretentiousness – every quarter it mailed out a new catalogue, taking orders for the *Emigré* T-shirt, the *Emigré* mouse-mat, the *Emigré* music sampler, the Zuzana Licko ceramic ampoule, all in a manner curiously and equally reminiscent of Shaker commerce and Fluxus elegance.

Then came the worldwide web and Emigre.com and then the first symptoms of altitude sickness. In Issue 40 (1996), entitled 'The Info Perplex', Diana Gromala, who directs a new media research laboratory at the University of Washington, wrote rather ominously:

> I have a number of students who regularly, though usually unwittingly, point out how strange our technologically mediated world can be. One clicks on the university's website – which has a video camera pointed on the main square of campus – to see if it is raining, rather than craning his neck to look out of the window, Another who admittedly is addicted to Nintendo games, tends to jump ever so slightly as he rounds corners of buildings. His body was conditioned by Nintendo games, where aggressive foes tend to lurk around corners. His body responds to both RL and the symbolic world of computer games confusing the two. My students are quick to ferret out technological X-files, quick to switch genders in their on-line communication, quick to devise ways to 'trip' in VR. One student has two distinct personalities – one on-line and one in RL – that she has sustained for more than five years. On a televised talk-show, she says, she'd have to appear as someone who suffers from a multiple personality disorder . . .

liquid

. . . I was going to go on to say that this last sentence of Diana Gromala's seemed to me to take the whole weightlessness thing to an untenable extreme, that it was difficult to see how a manufactured, mass-produced object despatched across the world in the holds of aeroplanes, inside beautifully labelled envelopes, could fend for itself for much longer in a culture in which the talk show experience was now to be regarded as RL, absolutely not VR. I was reminding myself that twice of late my subscription copies of *Emigré* had been delivered to me sopping wet as if fished up from the sea-bed I mentioned at the start, how I had complained to the British post office and that they had sworn virtually on the Bible that both must have been drenched already on arrival.

And then just this morning Issue 42 turned up here – my God! bone dry. No more VR. It is all about type and typography; there is even an essay about the old RL foundries; even reproductions of pages from old Monotype catalogues. Rudy says he is reinventing himself again; he is taking a gamble: 'First, we have opened the magazine to advertisers and have increased the presence of our own products. And second we have made the magazine free to anybody [in the USA] who has requested to be on the *Emigré* mailing list.'

One of the regulars, 'Mr Keedy', looks back over the digital revolution: 'The legacy of the last decade is a bizarre reconciliation evident in the new hybrid of "professional transgressors" who can be found in academia and advertising alike. Their work is on the cutting edge of a theoretical reality that moves faster than the speed of comprehension.'

O Zuzana! Too late!

Book Reviews

Experience or Interpretation: the Dilemma of Museums of Modern Art

Nicolas Serota
London: Thames & Hudson 1997.
63 pp. ISBN: 0 5 0055 02 98

As the subsidized art world pulls itself up straight, and attempts to batten down the hatches, in order to address the turbulence brought by Lottery-led development, Nicolas Serota's Walter Neurath lecture – *Experience or Interpretation* – raises some timely questions. Never before has there been so much money available for capital development. Never before has there been such self-imposed, and external, pressure to make the correct decisions. This comes after nearly thirty years of postmodernism, and at a time when curatorial debate is beginning to be informed by that of a culturally diverse society. The implications of the information revolution and digital technology are being absorbed and fewer unilateral tracks furrowed. A new government is fuelling, even if not yet proving, ideas of innovation, openness, social accountability and cohesion. Artists, have been, as they should, one step ahead of the curatorial establishment and have increasingly worked beyond the accepted conventions of gallery spaces, both in collaboration with curators and through independent artist-led initiatives. Art museums are founded on the culture of material objects. Metaphorically and morphologically they tend towards stasis, contemplation, even reverence. The cusp of change, the work of individual artists withstanding, is unfamiliar. As Serota asks, what is it that 'we expect from museums of modern art at the end of the twentieth century'?

In careful, scholarly fashion he traces the evolution of museum display, and in so doing questions the relationship of the museum both to contemporary production and to that, ubiquitous but ever elusive, individual, 'the viewer'. The story begins with Sir Charles Eastlake and his transformation of the National Gallery in the mid-nineteenth century from 'cabinet of treasures' to an edifying arrangement of works according to historical school. Such remained the model for the majority of public galleries until the 1980s, when the predominance of the curator, in determining the interpretation of the works (which was as likely as not to be in line with a canonical reading of modernist art history) was broken in favour of a set of more open interrelationships between artist, curator and viewer. Serota identifies this shift as the result of a change in the relationship between the work of art and the space in which it is shown, a move from the exclusivity of the studio as a place of work to more public arenas and an increasing awareness by artists (and by the art-going public) of the conventions of the museum itself. Illustrative examples are drawn from throughout the twentieth century, and range from Matisse's depiction, in *The Red Studio*, of his own work and workspace, through the purism of Mondrian and El Lissitzsky, the psychological and voyeuristic *mise-en-scène* of Duchamp and the downfall wrought by the minimalists on the accepted object/viewer hierarchy to Joseph Beuys's monumental and intensely personal series of rooms, *The Block*, in the Hessishees Landesmuseum, Darmstadt.

scale

A number of models are cited as responses to the vagaries of these relationships, between object, artist, curator, participant viewer and the physical and intellectual framework of the museum. At the Hallen für Neue Kunst in Scaffhausen, for example, open spaces replace separate rooms, so allowing the overlap of groups of work by individual artists to provoke the unpredictable and unexpected. Individual curators have adopted particular strategies for encouraging such reinterpretation. Rudi Fuchs, now at the Stedelijk Museum in Amsterdam, disperses to different parts of the museum key works by particular artists as roving catalysts. Jean Christophe Amman, at the architecturally dominant Museum für Moderne Kunst in Frankfurt, works, quote, 'from the perspective of my mind's eye', to encourage imaginative leaps and create 'climatic zones'. Odd functional spaces are, for example, turned into sites for commissioned artworks. Amongst what could easily become formulae for 'quick fixes', Serota acknowledges the importance of spaces and displays which encourage in-depth concentration and contemplation. All the cited approaches respond to the subtleties of postmodern readings. Emphasis is on the individual, the importance of 'discovery' and 'charting one's own path'.

The lecture admirably charts the history of the fine art museum within its own definitions. However, this definition is presented as unequivocal. No space is devoted to the rhetoric of display and its wider cultural origins or implications. Perhaps the greatest challenge to the art museum at the end of the twentieth century is to diffuse opacity, and to work with artists to do so.

sharp

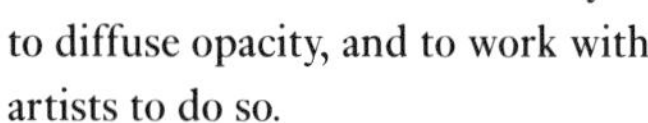

[Nicolas Serota is the Director of the Tate Gallery, London]

Hilary Gresty

Sensuality: essence and nonsense

Unknown Public (No. 8)
edited by John L. Walters
London: Laurence Ashton 1996

Finding audiences for new music other than mainstream pop, rock and jazz has always been problematic. While this is undoubtedly being addressed (through the education work of ensembles, and through the increasing eclecticism of festivals such as 'Meltdown' at the South Bank), the world of new music is still hampered by a certain determined factionalism, however those factions are defined (modernism versus postmodernism, 'new complexity' versus simplicity, avant-garde versus experimental).

Unknown Public attempts to avoid such boundaries, periodically issuing subscription CDs of 'creative music'. Quite what 'creative music' is remains unclear, probably deliberately – the important factor seems to be that the music included cannot (yet) be considered 'repertoire' and need not come from 'established' artists. The name *Unknown Public* seems positive in outlook (if slightly ironic, given its subscription basis); the implication is that the public is out there, somewhere, and the variety of musics included implies that the audience will be found and/or generated by the forging of links not necessarily based upon style but perhaps founded upon compositional approach, concept, or even simply a common relevance to the title of a particular issue. Each CD is packaged with relevant background information, comment, and letters in response to previous issues, and a web-site provides further information for potential listeners and contributors.

Issue 8, entitled 'sensuality: essence and nonsense', seeks to explore the relationship between music's sound and its sensual and/or intellectual content. The editorial avoids definitions of the kinds of music that may be considered sensual, and the appeal to immediacy is balanced by the recognition that intellectual content may contribute to that sensuality. However, the subscriber is also provided with a poster of responses to questions which seem to pose the problem in more oppositional terms: 'Must contemporary music always be "spiky" or "alienating"? Can new music evoke more pleasurable sensations without descending to banality? Can abstraction be sexy?' These questions are clearly designed to provoke, but nevertheless the implication is that the 'difficult' world of much contemporary classical (typically modernist) music may be at odds with a more deep-seated and more 'natural' desire for richly sonorous, immediately pleasurable soundworlds.

Of course, it could be argued that these polarities are being set up in order to be undermined by respondents and, more significantly, by the contents of the CD. This is the case to an extent; the fourteen tracks include a wide range of soundworlds and styles. Yet nearly all of the music belongs in some way to an essentially tonal tradition, whether it lies closer to the world of jazz, to the pop ballad, or to contemporary classical music. I stress the 'closer' here, for none of these terms gives a true sense of the proficiency with which the artists draw on a range of musical influences in order to create pieces that are not easily classifiable. The tape works of Sylvia Hallett and Fabienne Audéoud, different as they are, also rely on tonal centres, creating attractive, shimmering textures from a combination of drones, layered voices, ostinati, echoes and pulsations. Similarly, the extract from one of the most established composers included, Louis Andriessen, comprises slow, regular chords and rich extended harmonies, with semitonal dissonances in the vocal line used to pull against the basically tonal centre. Eddie McGuire's 'Romance' for guitar and 'cello is perhaps more demanding structurally, and requires detailed attention to timbral similarities and differences, but the material is again mainly based around the instruments' natural tonal resources (especially their natural harmonics and intervals of fifths and fourths).

It is (perhaps ironically) left to Mark-Anthony Turnage to represent the world of what could be described as mainstream contemporary classical music (by which I mean the kind of post-tonal music generally favoured by major orchestral and BBC commissions). Here we are presented with the sensuality of dissonance. Turnage's language is a rich amalgam of a classical post-tonal language with extended harmonies derived from his knowledge of jazz. The solo alto flute and soprano saxophone lines pull chromatically away from the chordal roots; Turnage's reference point is the painting of Francis Bacon, and the analogy with Bacon's painfully distorted images but sensuously rich colour is useful. The decision to include this piece, then, has the effect of opening up the question of musical sensuality, but as only one of the fourteen tracks the impact is limited. Aside from the Turnage, only Cathy Lane's 'Nesting Stones' explores texture in a framework that is not wholly tonally based; Lane's piece draws on many sounds and techniques familiar to the world of electroacoustic music (phase-vocoding, fragmenting, granulating), but provides both more personal and more universal resonances by using noises made by her daughter as the basic material.

This is neither to criticize the individual works, nor to accuse *Unknown Public* of promoting particular musical styles. Simply to be faced with a single CD which includes such a variety of vital new music is exciting, and the performances and recordings are of a very high standard (those of Howard Skempton's beautiful miniatures are particularly striking). But if the polarity of spiky/contemporary/intellectual versus sensual/pleasurable/immediate is really to be shown up as false (which I believe it should be), then it would be necessary to include other music which perhaps draws on aspects of that 'difficult' tradition, but which maybe has something to add to the debate. Some recent non-tonal music takes timbre as its primary focus, for example, creating sensual textural effects through what might otherwise be described as a modernist approach.

Beyond all this, though, is the fact that *Unknown Public* takes the not always accepted view that contemporary music exists in a vibrant cultural arena, wherein tastes should not be limited by affiliation to a particular style and where associations can be forged and explored on a whole range of bases: for this it is very welcome.

Catherine Laws

Paul McCarthy

Ralph Rugoff, Kristine Stiles, Giacinto Di Pietrantonio
London: Phaidon Press 1996.
160 pp. $29.95 pb
ISBN 0 7148 3552 8

Paul McCarthy's lurid work and Phaidon's lavish production values make for an extraordinary combination in this recent addition to Phaidon's series of monographs on contemporary artists. The series already includes books on Jeff Wall, Antony Gormley, Rachel Whiteread, Jessica Stockholder, Jimmie Durham and others. *Paul McCarthy* includes an interview by Kristine Stiles, articles by Ralph Rugoff and Giacinto Di Pietrantonio, and extracts from Sartre's *Nausea* chosen by McCarthy, a selection from McCarthy's own writings, a chronology and bibliography.

Rugoff provides a perceptive, comprehensive survey of McCarthy's context – the work of other body artists and the images of the mass media. Although Stiles seems to be talking at cross-purposes with McCarthy most of the time, they both have plenty of interesting observations to make in her interview. Di Pietrantonio makes an in-depth analysis of McCarthy's *Pinocchio Pipehose Household-dilemma*.

References to other artists and the imagery of Disney, Hollywood and TV are the language of McCarthy's work. He carries on both a dialogue with, and a spoof of, the work of other artists. His performances, videos and installations are littered with references to Pollock and de Kooning, the Viennese Actionists and other body artists including Pane, Paik and Acconci. McCarthy's *Inside Out, Olive Oil*, where he crawls through an enormous body frame, is reminiscent of Nikki de St Phalle's *Hon*; his *Face Painting – Floor, White Line* refers to Paik's *Zen for Head*; his *Contemporary Cure All* recalls Nitsch's bloody rituals and his cross-dressing and use of food-stuffs refer to Mühl. But McCarthy's work is Action Art without earnestness and Hollywood without frivolity. Art, popular culture, psychology, family values are all equally subject to his scathing mockery.

> I think my work deals with trauma, my experience of trauma, physical/mental trauma/abuse. I act as a clown stuffing and feeding orifices, enacting bodily hallucination – size changes, weight changes. Reality is force-fed: eat this. My actions are visceral; I want it to be visceral. The props of ketchup and mayonnaise are the right consistency for the action to be visceral. They cover the objects in a kind of body lubricant. They are force-fed into the mouth, the eye, the asshole.
> (Stiles 1996: 26)

His performances are recipes mixing diverse ingredients together. His body is the social body and on it he performs a messy autopsy on society. Rugoff points out that McCarthy's performance persona is a fluid signifying system, confronting the collection of contradictions that pass for a coherent self:

near

> a body whose borders were collapsing, whose insides seemed to be gushing out as though its thin bag of skin had ruptured.
> (Rugoff 1996: 33)

This is a vision that McCarthy shares with an increasing number of artists – Barney, Hatoum, Stelarc, Orlan, Gilbert & George, to name but a few – who are working with a queasy, visceral discourse in which the body is a leaky membrane between an individuated consciousness and the world. McCarthy uses prosthetics, costumes and makeup to exteriorize his insides, to inscribe them on the visible body. His body assumes an uncanny status as lifeless symbol, forced to eat and ingest images and values. Like the Ancient Greek theatre, McCarthy employs gigantic phalluses, scatological imagery, outrageous excess in a tragi-comedy of the pathology of normality. He uses props as a child manipulates dolls to create fantasy and comprehend reality, to picture the violence of social conditioning. McCarthy assumes 'the persona of a clownish and infantilizing host enacting a deranged educational programme' (Rugoff 1996: 32), drawing on the regressive imagery of Disney, Heidi, Pinocchio, clowns, hamburgers and ketchup. But McCarthy's infantilism and contaminated aesthetic, far from being an escape from reality, is a wide-eyed embrace of it. As Mary Douglas points out in *Purity and Danger*:

> Dirt was created by the differentiating activity of mind, it was a by-product of the creation of order . . . pollution symbols are as necessary as the use of black in any depiction whatsoever.
> (Douglas 1976: 160)

Tracey Warr

References

Douglas, Mary (1976) *Purity and Danger*, London: Routledge.

Rugoff, Ralph (1996) 'Survey', in *Paul McCarthy*, London: Phaidon.

Stiles, Kristine (1996) 'Interview', in *Paul McCarthy*, London: Phaidon.

Consciousness and the Actor

Daniel Meyer-Dinkgräfe
Frankfurt am Main, Berlin, Berne, New York, Paris, Vienna: Peter Lang, 1996. 167 pp.
ISBN 3-631-30143-X

What happens when someone performs? How does that performance affect its receivers? Are performers and audience changed by the experience? These basic questions have led investigators from Diderot to Barba to confront what Meyer-Dinkgräfe calls paradoxes, ranging from the simultaneous presence of involvement and detachment to the evocation of states beyond emotion and intellect. In order to explore and explain these states, many practitioners, especially since Artaud, have turned tentatively to India and the East: evidence of cultural piracy, postmodern eclecticism, or quest for a model of consciousness which could underpin both theory and practice? Meyer-Dinkgräfe turns it into the latter, courtesy of sharp analysis of the salient points of the 'paradoxes', an impressive reading of the *Natyashastra* and Sanskrit linguistics, and a thorough and lucid formulation of the requirements of such a model, which recognizes consciousness as psycho-physiological and locates its modes of possible operation both within and beyond existing eastern and western treatments of 'altered states'.

The notion of 'paradox' is to some extent undermined by the (appropriate) contextualization, which reveals it as a form of imprisonment within the paradigms of contemporary discourses. But this is a minor quibble compared with the challenge which the book delivers: to think outside the paradigm we currently operate. This does sometimes involve the reader in hard going, particularly in the detail of the Vedic Psychology model Meyer-Dinkgräfe outlines; but he marshals his diverse sources impressively and the force of the argument, that we need such a model to fully understand the aesthetics of performance and reception, is compelling. The resultant insights need to be tested against performance criteria; to do so will require a willingness to move outside the fixation with solely historicist modelling, or, in other words, to use theatre practice as an arena for experimentation of the full range of human resources.

Ralph Yarrow

Poems for the Millennium: The University of California Book of Modern and Post-modern Poetry

Jerome Rothenberg and Pierre Joris (eds)

Berkeley, CA: University of California Press, 1995. 811 pp.

ISBN: 0-520-07225-1 hb
ISBN: 0-520-07227-8 pb

This gigantic book is only the first of two volumes. Chronologically, it covers roughly the first half of the twentieth century, with significant forays made backwards in the direction of the nineteenth century and forwards into the postwar era. Structurally it is a hybrid. The more successful sub-sections are focused on -isms (Futurism, Surrealism, etc.; no separate Imagism, though) while the more problematic and longer subsections comprise samples of work by poets who seem more or less independent of the groupings specified elsewhere. Interspersed with the poetic material, which has a truly international range, is a series of free-form commentaries, which are sharply personal in tone and rhetorical complexion. Much of the poetic material has been freshly translated for this publication, and the translations are welcome. Among the texts that need no translation, a number represent their authors from a slightly unfamiliar angle, so that for several pages at a time the juxtapositions are enlivening and revisionary (I would say that this is particularly true of the 'Objectivists' section, in the selection of works by Zukofsky and Rakosi).

But despite the pleasures to be had locally, the book as a whole seems confused in its organizational principles. At frequent intervals, the commentaries make much of the historical occasion for writing, formulating, in various ways, the 'vital connection between history and language' (673). But historical context is at issue only in the design of those sections devoted to avant-garde groups, where the genuine interactions that produced a self-aware movement, or attracted the need for a label, are reflected in the repercussions of mutually informed texts. In the longer, eclectic sections entitled 'Galleries' ('A first Gallery', and so on) history is an inconvenience, getting in the way of highly personal dispositions for which the primary context is neither the occasion of composition, nor that of publication, but rather the moment of reception by the editors. This runaway subjectivism is particularly apparent in the final section entitled 'A book of Origins', which shouldn't be there. Although worthy in its intention of incorporating oral material and displaying an ethnological understanding of tradition to place against modernist doctrines, it is an arbitrary assortment, encompassing Confucius, Aboriginal sound poems and Bessie Smith. Any connections with either modernism or postmodernism are arguable, but the editors omit the argument; basically, their uncharacteristic reticence here provides Jerome Rothenberg with an opportunity to smuggle in a lifelong interest in 'ethnopoetics'.

Paradoxically, it is in the 'gallery' sections that historical raw data are in reasonable supply; the individual authors get individual commentaries inclusive of biographical and bibliographical information. This is not the case in the -ism sections, where the commentaries are disindividualizing. Most frustrating of all, very few poems indeed in this 800-page anthology are given dates of either composition or publication. In other words, this is not an anthology of poems in history, but a 'gallery' of portraits, or a group portrait of artistic heroes. The commentaries resort frequently to the use of the first person plural, and by this means they conscript the reader, or offer the reader membership of a trans-historical band of artistic innovators. On 193, for example, Futurism is cited as having sown 'the seeds of all that we were later to become'. The majority of readers will not be recruited in this way, and must understand the pronouns as referring to the editors themselves, and to people like them, in their capacity as heirs to a great tradition. The editorial vocabulary is inadvertently heroizing in its over-use of metaphors that physicalize the aesthetic project as a form of dynamic struggle. There is an excessive use of the word 'push' to refer to a variety of innovative agendas (e.g. on 521, 598, 678 and 706).

margin

In the end, the commentaries fuse together a performance of exclusion with attributions of universal value. The poems in between start to lose the connection with history that an anthology with scope like this could do much to explore.

Rod Mengham

Archive Review

The Robert Wilson Archives Byrd Hoffman Foundation New York

In 1961 Bob had invited me for the weekend to Waco, Texas, and took me around his hometown. There was not much to see, but he said: 'You have got to see the Robert Browning Memorial Library.' I wondered what the connection between Robert Browning and Waco was, but evidently some rich Texas lady had had a passion for Robert Browning's poetry and had persuaded her husband to buy manuscripts and memorabilia and to build this research library, which was also a shrine to Robert Browning. It is a wonderfully odd building, a neo-baroque structure right in the middle of Waco, where everything else is as far from Baroque as you can think. As you go in, to one side there is the library section with stained glass windows illustrating Browning's poems. To the other side there are rooms with memorabilia, odd things. I remember a room with glass cases with his fingernail brushes and scissors and some of his old shirts. The entrance hall is an enormous two-storey space with carved stones, and a big staircase going up.

minute

So Bob and I went in, it was a Saturday afternoon, and the place was absolutely empty, except that in the middle of the hall there was a big tea-table set up, with silver pots and cups and piles of cake and cookies and pastries. It was like Alice in Wonderland: you suddenly stumble upon a tea party. We started giggling and looked around, but we did not see anybody, and we wondered what this was all about. As we were just about to take a bite of cake, there suddenly was a voice from high above: 'Don't touch that, boys!', and a woman came down the staircase.[1]

This incident, as remembered by the poet, playwright, actor and scholar Paul Schmidt, may have initiated Robert Wilson's interest in archives. At the time, 20-year-old Wilson was studying business and law at the University of Texas at Austin. A year later he moved to New York and, in 1966, graduated from Pratt Institute with a degree in interior design. After acquiring a loft in SoHo and performing a few solo pieces, he founded a theatre group called the Byrd Hoffman School of Byrds, named in honour of his Waco dance teacher. In 1968, in order to organize the activities of the group and raise funds for its activities, Wilson established the Byrd Hoffman Foundation (BHF). Besides co-ordinating workshops and classes, theatre and gallery presentations and a project to purchase land and construct a studio space for a summer school, the purpose of the BHF was, from the beginning, to document the work of the group and its leader, Robert Wilson, on film and in notebook publications, and to maintain an archive.[2]

Today, after thirty years of work in theatre, opera, film and the visual arts, and after almost a hundred theatre productions on five continents, Wilson's archival materials have amounted to over 500 cubic feet (14 cubic metres).[3] They continue to grow, since Wilson is a living and ever more productive artist in several fields. And he is very conscious of the importance and difficulties of preserving remains of the ephemeral art of theatre. His travelling office accompanies him around the globe in a few sturdy bags, carried and managed by a personal assistant, and in it there is a folder labelled 'archive'. Each day it is filled with documents related to his life and work: letters and postcards; personal photographs; scripts and books; newspaper clippings and magazines. His contracts demand that the final production is videotaped and photographed for the archive and that a set of press clippings is prepared for him. The assistants are advised to label and sort the many table sketches he produces during rehearsals and work sessions with his collaborators. Multiple copies of programme books, press kits, posters and flyers are gathered as well. Almost nothing gets thrown away, and his archivist has to try hard to catch up with new documents coming in every day. Nevertheless, the BHF archive gladly accepts donations of press clippings or other material relating to Wilson's work.

Special handling is required for three-dimensional artefacts which Wilson considers artworks with a market value. After a production has closed, he tries to secure as many of the stage props and furniture pieces as possible, because he regards them as sculptures.[4] Most of the large charcoal drawings he produces during and after the work on a play do not end up in the archive. They

Performance Research 2(3), pp.110-115 © Routledge 1997

are reproduced in the programme books (which double-function as art catalogues), are exhibited in local galleries alongside the opening of the play, and are later handled by his primary art agent, the Paula Cooper Gallery in New York.[5] Many of the drawings and sculptures by Wilson have been acquired by private collectors and public institutions.[6]

Wilson never was an artist in residence or artistic director of a theatre but always worked as an independent director and designer, both in his early years producing his own plays and, from 1984 on, when commissioned to direct plays and operas from repertory in European and American theatres. So he could never rely on a theatre to keep his archive. And although he has taught acting and directed students in drama departments, he has never held a tenured position in an academic institution that would preserve his papers. But when the School of Byrds dissolved in the mid-1970s, Wilson kept the administrative structure of the BHF to manage his works, and assigned the task of archivist to one of the changing members of his staff. Each one of them developed their own system to cope with the increasing number of documents, until, in 1995, Geoffrey Wexler became the first professionally trained archivist.

There is no single Robert Wilson Archive any more. Wexler's predecessors have dealt with space and staff limitations by giving selected parts of the archive to two academic theatre collections where the materials are professionally stored and accessible to researchers:

- the Harvard Theatre Collection at Harvard, Cambridge MA
- the Rare Books and Manuscripts Library at Columbia University, New York City.

The Harvard Theatre Collection at the Harvard College Library in Cambridge, Massachusetts,[7] received materials from 1978 to 1986 at the recommendation of the late George Ashley, a Harvard alumnus, who was an early associate of Robert Wilson and one of the first administrators of the BHF. The 'Robert Wilson Collection' contains mainly: a fairly complete series of play and exhibition posters from 1969 to 1984; press notices and clippings from 1964 to 1984; administrative files of the BHF from 1971 to1982; a few playscripts and programme books; production tapes for the video installation *Spaceman* (1976) and the video film *Stations* (1982); and a video recording of the 12-hour play *The Life and Times of Joseph Stalin* (1973). Except for the administrative files and the video production tapes, duplicates of the material can be found at either the BHF or Columbia University.

The Rare Books and Manuscripts Library of the Columbia University, New York,[8] has a collection of 'Robert Wilson Papers' ranging from 1969 to 1992. According to the official statistics, it is 148 linear feet (45 metres) in size and contains 'ca. 149,000 items in 292 boxes, 1 phonodisc, 1 audiocassette, 15 oversize folders, 3 scrapbooks and 108 posters'. The materials are a gift by Robert Wilson and the BHF which was arranged by the late Dallas Pratt, professor of psychology at Columbia and an early member of the Byrd Hoffman School of Byrds. In 1988, most of the old administrative and production files of the BHF were transferred to Columbia, where the librarians kept the documents in their original manila folders but rearranged them by new categories.

There are: a box with cataloged and arranged correspondence (among them letters by Wilson collaborators and by artist friends like Eugene Ionesco, Jasper Johns, Kenneth King, and Jessye Norman); 20 boxes with files concerning the BHF administration, early activities of Wilson and the Byrds (theatre, dance, film, gallery, performance presentations at their loft and elsewhere), early publications (among them typescripts of unpublished interviews with Wilson and the Byrds), works not completed, and Wilson's address books and calendars from the 1970s; 200 boxes with files pertaining to specific theatre productions, complete until 1988, in alphabetical order (e.g. 13 boxes on the landmark opera *Einstein on the Beach* and 60 boxes alone documenting *the CIVIL warS*, Wilson's only partly successful attempt to produce in six countries a theatrical epic for the1984 Cultural Olympics); 20 boxes with research files and material for new and suspended projects (among them new operas with Philip Glass and early attempts to stage *King Lear* and *Pelléas*); 10 boxes with files relating to video projects (*Spaceman*, *Stations*, and *Video 50*); 5 boxes with documents of art projects (exhibition invitations, catalogues and press); 30 boxes with almost complete press clippings from 1964 to 1987; a box with a taped radio interview and a few

detail

slides; 6 boxes with printed material (books, programme books, magazine articles); map-cases with play and exhibition posters (similar but not identical to the Harvard collection); 25 boxes with miscellaneous contracts, financial records and written and faxed correspondence; and 1 box documenting the imprisonment of Wilson in Crete 1972 for the possession of hashish and the successful international release efforts.

A finding aid (which is available online[9]) lists the box and folder titles, but the huge number of papers in the folders has not yet been catalogued, which makes research a slow and sometimes surprising process. Not more than four of the boxes can be paged at a time. After a short wait they are brought to the glass-enclosed and air-conditioned rare manuscripts reading room, where work conditions are strict but pleasant. Wilson's papers are treated no differently from other treasures of the collection: medieval manuscripts, incunabula, a first folio of Shakespeare's plays, a drawing by Galilei, diaries of George Washington, a manuscript of Poe's last poem, an autograph of Bruckner's Seventh Symphony or the collected papers of the poet Hart Crane. None of the materials circulates, but photocopies can be made on request.

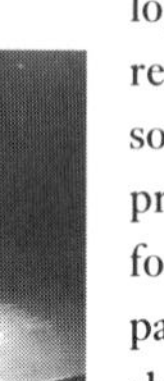

very

Two institutions hold copies of videos documenting some of Wilson's theatre productions: the *New York Public Library for the Performing Arts*[10] and the *Institut für Angewandte Theaterwissenschaft*[11] in Gießen, Germany. All videos are duplicates of tapes in the BHF collection.

The major portion of the Wilson archive is still part of the *Byrd Hoffman Foundation* office in New York,[12] a rather small office, effectively designed by Wilson himself, on the ninth floor, high above the Holland tunnel traffic, with a great view over SoHo. Sanded glass walls partition the space into cubicles and allow soft natural light into the interior parts. A row of hip-high filing cabinets allows for easy access and there is a large temporary working table. A few beautiful objects from Wilson's private collection (glass vases, Indonesian sculptures, a light-blue goose, etc.) are arranged to create a quiet and smooth work atmosphere. Archival materials are kept in tidy rows of grey boxes on wood and glass shelves. The most important and valuable materials are kept here, documenting all of Wilson's works in theatre, video and the visual arts. Since the office is active and Wilson is an artist for whom work and life are identical, most business and private records are not yet open for research. Geoffrey Wexler, the new archivist, is creating a computer-based finding aid and has arranged the research section into the following categories.

The collection of about 10,000 photographs is arranged by production and consists of monochrome prints, colour prints and contact sheets of performances and rehearsals. Compared with the work of other directors and designers, Wilson's work has always been extremely compelling visually and attractive to photographers. But since he could rarely afford his own photographer, his productions were documented in many different styles, and the photos vary in quality. There are only a few photos of Wilson's early performances. Most of the first large-scale works with the Byrds are well represented, but no photographer was able fully to capture the 7-day play *Ka Mountain* in Shiraz or the 24-hour play *Overture* in Paris, both in 1972. When Wilson started to produce his works in European theatres, they were documented by staff and press photographers. However, the BHF archive does not always hold the best shots. Currently, the archive is actively seeking to acquire photographs and to fill in the gaps.

Another partition of the photo archive documents Wilson's two- and three-dimensional artworks: as individual drawings, prints, photographs and sculptures, and in the spatial context of exhibitions and installations. In addition, there are portraits of Robert Wilson and his collaborators, some of them taken by prominent photographers like Horst P. Horst, Peter Hujar, Robert Mapplethorpe and Duane Michals, some others going back to his childhood days. A series of slides is organized in the same way as the photographs and, in addition, has a section with slides that were used in productions such as *Curious George* (1979) or the *Knee Plays* (1984). Books and articles about Wilson are arranged by production, or, if more general in scope, by year. Part of the book section contains dissertations and other scholarly works about Wilson, if sent to the archive. Another section covers the press about exhibitions and installations. The programmes series contains programme books, playbills, posters and other promotional materials for each of some eighty theatre productions, plus some for performances, lectures, video presentations, etc.; in addition, there are catalogues, flyers and invitations to exhibitions and installations. A few of the original artworks by Wilson are also stored or displayed in the archive, among them charcoal drawings and prints and chair sculptures like the *Einstein Chair* or a chair for *Doctor Faustus Lights the Lights*, miniature versions of a marble sofa for *Danton's Death* or a granite bench for *Erwartung*.

The section of the archive not directly accessible for research contains a collection of filmed and videotaped performances, rehearsals, interviews and films by Wilson, including filmed footage from early performances, the 7-day play mentioned above, and lectures that Wilson has given internationally. Selected tapes can be borrowed from the archive, which also holds a few sound recordings, mostly reel-to-reel production tapes for sound effects in the plays. Wilson's research library in the archive includes books about theatre, art, biographies of artists and protagonists of his plays, literature and poetry, many of them with dedications. Often, when Wilson is working in a faraway theatre and has a question, the archivist becomes a researcher and looks for information, both in the library and the production files. These are opened when an initial idea for a theatre or art project arises and are kept open until the project has been either fully realized or abandoned. They consist of artistic, production and financial files, and Wilson frequently refers to them, modifying an idea or reassembling a creative team. Correspondence with friends and collaborators (Heiner Müller, Philip Glass, Eugène Ionesco, Jerome Robbins *et al.*) is filed separately, as are the corporate records of the BHF and other corporations Wilson is involved in. In recent years, Wilson has started to collect art, both by renowned visual artists and by craftsmen around the world (baskets from Indonesia, masks from India, pottery from Germany, chairs from everywhere), and the records of his private art collection are kept in the archive. Since he was named executor of the estate of artist Paul Thek, some of Thek's works and papers are also stored here. Not open to researchers are some of Wilson's private papers, notebooks and his private photo collection.

There are very few theatre artists of such importance who have had the traces of their work preserved better and more completely than Wilson, so his archives have been the object of growing scholarly interest. The first dissertation based on research in the archives appeared as early as 1980,[13] and in recent months several books exploring parts of the archives have appeared.[14] For a short time, the BHF has maintained a Robert Wilson website on the Internet[15] with short descriptions about selected plays, a complete list of theatre works and art exhibitions, an extensive bibliography of books, articles and reviews, and contact information for all Wilson archives and video distributors. In the future, a database about the materials in the archive will be added. The website will also be the home of an informal Robert Wilson researcher's network, co-ordinated by the author. One of the purposes will be further to enrich the archive by collecting press clippings worldwide, by encouraging student interns in productions to write production notes and by attempting to secure even more traces of Wilson productions (such as original drops and other set parts).

Arguably the most fruitful use of the archives to date was made by multimedia artist Paul Kaiser who combined early film footage, sketches, notes and a recently filmed interview with Wilson to create a CD-ROM visualizing Wilson's development of a theatrical language between 1967 and 1976.[16]

There are plans to reunite all parts of the archives, together with a permanent exhibition of Wilson's art, in Watermill Center, a renovated laboratory building in eastern Long Island, where Wilson holds workshops with artists and students during the summer. Whether these plans can be realized and make sense remains to be discussed. As long as Wilson is alive and productive, the archives will be not only a repository for the past, but also a source for new works. For Wilson, the veritable archive for the art of the ephemeral is elsewhere:

> You cannot put a theatre performance on the wall or in a bookshelf. This troubles me. But it is the nature of my work that it continues to exist only in the memories of people. And that is the beauty of it.[17]

Jan Linders

• **Byrd Hoffman Foundation: photo and programme archive**
Photo: Rica Linders

• Byrd Hoffman Foundation: private art collection and miniature sculptures. Photo: Rica Linders

Notes

1 Interview with the author, September 1994.

2 Cf. the annual report of the Byrd Hoffman Foundation, October 1970. Columbia University, Rare Books and Manuscripts Library, Robert Wilson Papers, Box 11: Byrd Hoffman School of Byrds —Activities.

3 Most facts in this article were gathered in interview with archivist Geoffrey Wexler, April 1997.

4 Some chair sculptures have been produced and sold in a limited edition.

5 Paula Cooper Gallery, 534 West 21st Street, New York, NY 10011. Tel. +1-212 255.1105. Fax +1-212 255.5156.

6 Among the public collections holding artworks by Robert Wilson are: the Art Institute of Chicago; the Centre Georges Pompidou, Paris; the Cooper-Hewitt Museum, New York; the Kunstmuseum, Berne; the Menil Collection, Houston; the Metropolitan Museum of Art, New York; Museum Boymans van Beuningen, Rotterdam; the Museum of Contemporary Art, Los Angeles; the Museum of Fine Arts, Boston; the Museum of Fine Arts, Houston; the Museum of Modern Art, New York; the Philadelphia Museum of Art, Philadelphia; the Stedelijk Museum, Amsterdam; and the Walker Art Center, Minneapolis. For further locations consult the Wilson website mentioned below.

7 Robert Wilson Collection, Harvard Theatre Collection, The Curator [Jeanne Newlin], Harvard College Library, Cambridge, MA 02138. Tel. +1-617 495.2445. Fax: +1-617 496.5786. The collection cannot be used without the written permission of the Byrd Hoffman Foundation (see address and telephone number below).

8 Robert Wilson Papers, Rare Book and Manuscripts Library, Curator of

Manuscripts [Bernard Crystal], Butler Library, Sixth Floor, East Columbia University, 535 West 114th Street, New York, NY 10027. Tel. +1-212 854.3528. Fax: +1-212 854.1365. The collection is open to all researchers without appointment; the viewing of a few documents requires approval of the Byrd Hoffman Foundation (address below).

9 http://www.columbia.edu/cu/libraries/indiv/rare/guides/Wilson, R/main.html

10 New York Public Library for the Performing Arts, Theater on Film and Tape Archives, New York Public Library for the Performing Arts, Lincoln Center, 111 Amsterdam Avenue, New York, NY 10023. Tel. +1-212 870.1641. The collection contains videotapes of several important Wilson productions, including *Einstein on the Beach* (BAM, 1984), *the CIVIL warS* – Rome Section (BAM, 1987), *the CIVIL warS* – Cologne Section (American Repertory Theatre, 1985), *Robert Wilson and the CIVIL warS* (documentary by Howard Brookner, 1985), *The Golden Windows* (BAM, 1985), *The Forest* (BAM 1988), *When We Dead Awaken* (American Repertory Theatre, 1991), and *The Making of a Monologue: Robert Wilson's Hamlet*, (documentary by Marion Kessel 1995). The materials are available to the general public. The videotapes do not circulate, but viewing facilities are provided in the library.

11 Institut für Angewandte Theaterwissenschaft [Professor Dr Helga Finter], Justus-Liebig-Universität Gießen, Karl-Glöckner-Strasse 21a 35394, Gießen, Germany. Tel. +49-641 702.2381. Fax. +49-641 702.5300. Begun by Dr Andrzej Wirth, the Gießen collection contains extensive archival and videotape documentation of Robert Wilson's works. The collection is available by appointment only.

12 Robert Wilson Archive, The Archivist [Geoffrey Wexler], Byrd Hoffman Foundation, 131 Varick Street, Suite 908, New York, NY 10013. Tel. +1-212 620.0220. Fax. +1-212 627.0129. The archive is open by appointment only. Materials do not circulate, but limited space for research is available at the office.

13 Luiz Roberto Galizia, 'Robert Wilson's creative processes: whole works of art for the contemporary American theatre', PhD thesis, University of California at Berkeley, 1980. Typescript in Columbia University archive, Box 17: books file.

14 Arthur Holmberg, *The Theatre of Robert Wilson*, 'Directors in Perspective' series (Cambridge, New York and Melbourne: Cambridge University Press, 1996). Manfred Böhm and Minu Sharegi (eds) *Robert Wilson* (Hamburg: Kämpfer Verlag, 1996). Holm Keller, *Robert Wilson* , 'Regie im Theater' series (Frankfurt am Main: Fischer Taschenbuch Verlag, 1997). Franco Bertoni, *Robert Wilson. Scenografie e installazioni* (Florence: Octavo, 1997). Jan Linders and Grischa Meyer (eds) *Robert Wilson Theatre Work* (New York and Berlin: G+B Arts/Verlag der Kunst, 1998).

15 http://www.robertwilson.com

16 Paul Kaiser, *Robert Wilson: A Visionary of Theatre*, produced by Riverbed, Inc., New York. For information about publication contact http://www.riverbed.com.

17 Cf. interview with Gabriele Henkel, 'Wer nicht hören will, muß sehen', *Die Erste* (Magazin für das Deutsche Schauspielhaus Hamburg) 4 (May/June 1986).

Performance Research: On Refuge

Notes on Contributors

THE EDITORS

Ric Allsopp is a joint editor of *Performance Research* and issue editor for On Refuge. He is co-founder of Writing Research Associates, an international partnership organizing, promoting and publishing performance. He is currently a research fellow at Dartington College of Arts. He has been a research associate with the Centre for Performance Research since 1986, and has been associated with the School for New Dance Development, Amsterdam since 1990.

Richard Gough is general editor of *Performance Research*. He is senior research fellow in the Department of Theatre, Film and Television Studies at the University of Wales, Aberystwyth and Artistic Director of the Centre of Performance Research (CPR), the successor of Cardiff Laboratory Theatre, of which he was a founder member. He edited *The Secret Art of the Performer* (London: Routledge, 1990) and has curated and organized numerous conference and workshop events over the last twenty years as well as directing and lecturing internationally.

Claire MacDonald is a joint editor of *Performance Research* and issue editor for On Refuge. She is a writer and critic and is currently completing a book on feminism and performance art for Routledge. She was head of Theatre at Dartington College of Arts 1987–9 and is now senior lecturer and research fellow in theatre at De Montfort University in Leicester, UK. She was a founder member of Impact Theatre and Insomniac Theatre companies and has written performance texts and librettos for many productions, including, most recently, the script for the music theatre piece *Beulah Land* (London, ICA, 1994).

CONTRIBUTORS

Philip Auslander is an Associate Professor in the School of Literature, Communication and Culture of the Georgia Institute of Technology, Atlanta, Georgia, USA. He writes on theoretical and cultural approaches to performance and teaches in the areas of Performance Studies, Media Studies and Cultural Studies. The working title of his current project is *Liveness: Performance in a Mediatized Culture*.

Marcia Blumberg is a Visiting Research Fellow at the Open University on a post-doctoral fellowship from the Social Sciences and Humanities Research Council of Canada, working on diverse stagings and representations of AIDS. In 1996 she worked as a Research Fellow in South African Theatre at the Open University. She is co-editing with Dennis Walder *South African Theatre As/And Intervention* and is completing a book, *Engendering Intervention in Contemporary South African Theatre*. She taught in the English department at York University, Toronto and has published widely on contemporary theatre, in particular the plays of Athol Fugard.

Roger Bourke and Danielle Faggio are artists working with video, sound and interactive technologies and collaborating on a series of installations enquiring into sensory and perceptual 'slippage and disturbance' which respond to the physical presence of the viewer within the work. *Liquid Rapture* is a video and sound installation first shown in Poznan, Poland in 1997.

desperate optimists are Christine Molloy and Joe Lawlor. Hailing from Dublin, Ireland they have lived and worked in England since 1987. In 1992 they set up the company desperate optimists. Since their first production, *Anatomy of Two Exiles* (1992) they have been developing work through residencies and commissions and have toured internationally with *Hope* (1993), *Dedicated* (1995) and *Indulgence* (1996). They are currently working on a new touring production *Stalking Realness* (1997) and a short film for the Blipvert project.

Arnold Dreyblatt, artist and composer, born in 1953, studied film and video art and music composition. He has been developing interactive installations and performances involving texts, images and sound over the last twenty years. He has been based in Europe since 1984 and is presently living in Berlin and continuing work on 'Memory Arena' and related projects. More information can be found at: www.uni-lueneburg.de/memory/

Hilary Gresty works as a freelance consultant, writer and researcher. She is part-time Director of the Visual Arts and Galleries Association, the representative body for visual arts organizations concerned with contemporary practice. She was formerly Curator at Kettle's Yard, University of Cambridge.

Rudi Laermans is Senior Lecturer in the Department of Sociology of the Catholic University in Leuven, Belgium. He has written widely on contemporary performance, in particular on the work of Needcompany (Jan Lauwers) and Damaged Goods (Meg Stuart).

Kirsten Lavers is an installation artist. She has recently completed a series of 10 site specific works in England and Northern Ireland in collaboration with Melanie Thompson as The Zwillinge Project. Kirsten also makes artists books, solo installation/performance works and is a co-editor of Var, a magazine on the World Wide Web. She teaches regularly at Dartington College of Arts and De Montfort University and for the past four years has been responsible for the installation and management of emergency winter shelters for homeless people.

Catherine Laws has just left the post of Subject Leader for Music at De Montfort University, Leicester, in order to lecture at Dartington College of Arts. She is a pianist and lecturer specializing in contemporary music and inter-disciplinary work in the performing arts.

Jan Linders, dramaturg, director and writer, is living and lecturing in Hamburg. He is currently editing a 400-page work booklet entitled 'Robert Wilson Theatre Work' to be published in early 1998 by G. & B. Arts, New York/Harwood Academic Publishers, London.

Rod Mengham lectures at the University of Cambridge where he is a Fellow of and Director of Studies in English at Jesus College.

Kevin Mount edits and designs publications for Dartington Social Research Unit, part of Bristol University's School for Policy Studies.

Andrea Phillips is Lecturer in Visual Performance at Dartington College of Arts, UK and works as a freelance editor and performance critic.

Andrew Quick is Lecturer in Theatre Studies at Lancaster University, UK. He has written on Forced Entertainment and the sublime in *Contemporary Theatre Review* and is currently preparing a book on the politics of experimentation.

Alan Read is author of *Theatre and Everyday Life: an Ethics of Performance*. He is currently Professor and Chair of Drama and Theatre Studies at Roehampton Institute. Between 1994 and 1997 he was Director of Talks at the Institute of Contemporary Arts in London.

Valentina Valentini, a scholar of the problems of performance in the twentieth century, teaches performance studies at the Art Department of the University of Calabria. She is a leading authority on performance and multimedia events and her work has been published in many specialists magazines including Biblioteca Teatrale, The Drama Review, Drammaturgia and Performance Arts Journal.

Marc von Henning translates, writes and directs for theatre. *THEATREMACHINE*, his translations of theatre texts by the late German playwright Heiner Müller, is published by Faber & Faber. He has translated *First Ladies* by Werner Schwab for the Royal Court, to be seen in December 1997. For his own company, p r i m i t i v e s c i e n c e, he has written and directed *Hunger* (1994–5), *Spell* (1995) and *Imperfect Librarian* (1996), all performed at the Slaughterhouse, the Young Vic Theatre and the Purcell Room, Royal Festival Hall. *After the Hunt* was performed at Spital studio before invited audiences. He lives and works in London.

Aaron Williamson is a performance writer who works with new ideas about language and communication from the perspective of his own deafness. He is a research fellow at Dartington College of Arts; publications include *A Holy Throat Symposium* (1993).

Kirsten Winderlich is an artist living and working in Latvia.

Krzysztof Wodizcko is a visual artist born in Warsaw and living in New York City. He is currently Head of Research into Interrogative Design at the Massachusetts Institute of Technology.

Tracey Warr is a Researcher in Public and Site Specific Art at the Surrey Institute of Art and Design.

Ralph Yarrow teaches drama at the University of East Anglia where he has been Chair both of Drama and French. He writes, directs and performs in a variety of languages and locations, and recently published *Consciousness, Literature and Theatre: Theory and Beyond* (1997) with Peter Malekin.

the LIBRARY

Dec 20th 1996 - April 12th 1997

Nightly 7pm - 9.30am

free to anyone who would otherwise have to sleep roug

25 army beds + mattresses
50 sleeping bags
100 blankets
30 pillows
tables + chairs
television
kitchen equipment
2 fridges
1 washing machine
1 tumble drier
miscellaneous warm clothing
first aid kit
CCTV system
intercom door release system
smoke detection and emergency lighting system

staff team of 10

Funded by:
City Council Revenue Services
Local and National Charities

1 book